Evangelical Christian Education

Evangelical Christian Education

Mid-Twentieth-Century Foundational Texts

Fernando Arzola Jr.

Foreword by
Kevin E. Lawson

WIPF & STOCK · Eugene, Oregon

EVANGELICAL CHRISTIAN EDUCATION
Mid-Twentieth-Century Foundational Texts

Copyright © 2014 Fernando Arzola Jr. All rights reserved. Except for brief quotations in critical publications or reviews, no part of this book may be reproduced in any manner without prior written permission from the publisher. Write: Permissions, Wipf and Stock Publishers, 199 W. 8th Ave., Suite 3, Eugene, OR 97401.

Wipf & Stock
An imprint of Wipf and Stock Publishers
199 W. 8th Ave., Suite 3
Eugene, OR 97401

www.wipfandstock.com

ISBN 13: 978-1-62564-596-8

Manufactured in the U.S.A.

Contents

Foreword by Kevin E. Lawson | vii
Preface | xiii
Acknowledgments | xv
Permissions | xvii

1 Charles B. Eavey: *Principles of Teaching for Christian Teachers* (1940) | 1
2 Frank E. Gaebelein: *Christian Education in a Democracy* (1951) | 27
3 Findley B. Edge: *Teaching for Results* (1956) | 48
4 Lois E. LeBar: *Education That Is Christian* (1958) | 60
5 Lawrence O. Richards: *Creative Bible Teaching* (1970) | 85

Bibliography | 99

Foreword

Why, in the early years of the twenty-first century, should anyone read a book of "foundational texts" on evangelical Christian education from the mid-twentieth century? Why indeed?

When it comes to the study of ministry practices, the church in America today has a tendency of being fairly ahistorical in outlook. That is, we are not very interested in looking at ministry practices of the past, or older writings about good ministry practice. Instead, we tend to focus on the immediate needs around us, and design ministry practices from scratch to address those needs. It seldom occurs to us that others in the past may have faced similar needs and developed ministry approaches that we might learn from. How near-sighted can we be?

Perhaps it is due to our pride and arrogance. This myopic approach to ministry cuts us off from the valuable insights of those who have gone before us. Many of yesterday's leaders and writers have much to teach us about what is important, how to pursue it, and what to avoid. We are not the first to wrestle with issues of educational ministry effectiveness, nor shall we be the last. We would do well to consider what our "older brothers and sisters" have to teach us about good Christian education practice. We may be surprised at how relevant their ideas and insights are for the challenges we face today.

In this volume, Fred Arzola has collected together excerpts from some of the "foundations" of evangelical Christian education writings from the mid-twentieth century. This was an important time for the evangelical Protestant church movement as it sought to develop stronger educational ministry models in response to poor educational practices of the past, disagreements with the older liberal

Foreword

models of religious education of the early twentieth century, and perceived deficiencies in the newer "neo-orthodox" approaches that were then being developed. A little background on evangelical Christian education efforts and developments in this time period may help set a context for appreciating the writings presented in this book.

Background on Evangelical Christian Education in the Mid-Twentieth Century

The early part of the twentieth century saw evangelical leadership in educational ministry marginalized with the growing influence of the liberal theological approach to religious education. Evangelicals, who had previously played an active part in national and international collaborative efforts like international Sunday School conferences, became less involved in the modern religious education movement and more isolated. This began to change in the early 1930s with the formation of the Evangelical Teacher Training Association. More cooperative efforts among evangelicals were soon to follow. In 1939 a group of evangelical publishers met to discuss issues related to the Uniform Lesson series produced under the auspices of the International Council of Religious Education. Their concerns centered on the liberal theology, progressive educational approach, social gospel teaching, and the limited biblical content in these materials. This meeting has been characterized as a "protest meeting," and though the group took no action, it showed the need for an evangelical organization to address these concerns and provide alternate resources.[1]

In 1942 the National Association of Evangelicals (NAE) was formed. This organization grew rapidly and quickly turned its attention to efforts of cooperation in Christian education. In 1944, at a meeting of the Church School Commission of the NAE attended by independent publishers, denominational publishers and editors, and leaders of interdenominational and nondenominational organizations, it was decided to develop a new organization to reinvigorate the work of the Sunday School and produce new uniform Sunday School lesson outlines that reflected evangelical beliefs. At conferences in 1945 and 1946, the National Sunday School Association (NSSA)

1. Eavey, *History of Christian Education*, 295.

was established as an affiliate of the NAE. Its purposes included the revitalization of the Sunday School, promotion of the study of the Bible, fostering Sunday School conventions, and the publication of resources in support of evangelical Christian education. Its new uniform lesson materials were used by several evangelical publishers to provide curricula for an estimated one million pupils across the United States when they were begun in 1948, and by over three million pupils by 1964.[2]

The NSSA began holding annual national conventions in 1946 and these grew rapidly for over a decade. Regional conferences were also developed, and these grew to the point where attendance at the national conferences was negatively affected. "By 1960, NSSA maintained 21 affiliated city Sunday school associations, 17 area associations and 8 state associations."[3] Though the primary emphasis was on equipping Sunday School volunteers, these conferences quickly expanded their focus to include lay people involved in other educational ministries as well. In addition, during the 1950s and 60s the NSSA developed several commissions focused on specific areas of Christian education, including the Research Commission (1951), the Camp Commission, the Youth Commission, the Denominational Sunday School Secretaries, the Area Chairman Commission, and the affiliated group the National Association of Directors of Christian Education.[4] The Research Commission eventually became the Society of Professors in Christian Education (SPCE), an evangelical counterpart to the theologically and religiously broader Religious Education Association (REA), an association of professors, practitioners, and researchers in religious education.

This active time period, the 1940s through the 60s, is when the five excerpts of this book were written. Evangelicals, though a minority in the religious education scene, were collaborating to develop alternate teaching materials and strengthen teaching practices across denominational lines. As they looked around them, they saw weak and at times harmful pedagogical practices within the evangelical church. These leaders shared a number of convictions about

---

2. Ibid., 296–97.
3. Shelley, *Evangelicalism in America*, 96.
4. Ibid.

Foreword

the nature and importance of the Scriptures, the work of the Holy Spirit to teach and transform followers of Christ, and the importance of active teaching and learning methods. They shared a vision to challenge and equip those who taught the Bible in the church and parachurch settings to teach the truths of Scripture in relevant and impactful ways. This motivated them to write the excerpts you are about to read.

Selecting the "Foundational Texts"

It is quite a challenge to select the "foundational texts" from the range of authors and writings of this time period, and I don't envy Fred in his efforts to determine what to include and what to leave out. In addition to the books and authors selected for this volume, some editors might have considered works by James DeForest Murch, Harold Mason, or Mary LeBar. Others might have considered writings by LeRoy Ford, Herbert Byrne, or Donald Joy. If space permitted, it would have been easy to justify the inclusion of others beyond these five.

I agree that the five authors and excerpts that are included in this text are indeed the "foundations" of this time period. These works helped shape a generation of Christian education ministry leaders like myself, helping us to identify worthy teaching goals and effective teaching methods, and showing us the importance of really knowing our students well so we could teach them as an act of love. Their influence was broad and extended over the course of many years. Together, they reflect the concerns of evangelical educational ministry leaders and their insights both on what made for good teaching and what one had to do to become effective in teaching the Bible—in ways that could be used by God to bring about real transformation among those who sought to follow Christ as Lord and Savior. These excerpts will whet your appetite to read more. In addition, I think you will see how in many ways some of the teaching practices of the present are responses to concerns first raised by these authors decades ago—"echoes" of their call for increased effectiveness in our teaching of the Bible. On the other hand, you may find

Foreword

yourself shaking your head a bit because some of the concerns noted then are still with us today.

It is my hope that you will find yourself motivated and challenged by what you read. We may have unique challenges in our contexts today, but many of the same principles and priorities written to address the needs of the church then also apply in our current teaching ministries. Thank you, Fred, for making these writings available to a new generation.

Dr. Kevin E. Lawson
Director, PhD and EdD programs in Educational Studies,
Talbot School of Theology, Biola University
Editor, *Christian Education Journal* (www.biola.edu/cej)
Editor, Christian Educators of the 20th Century Project (www.christianeducators20.com)

Preface

Aim and Hope

This aim of this book is to present five mid-twentieth-century foundational texts in modern evangelical Christian education. My hope is that this book will 1) present seminal texts that have significantly impacted the field of evangelical Christian education, 2) inspire readers to further examine the writings of the leading figures of modern evangelical Christian education, and 3) help to broaden and deepen the reader's theological and educational worldview in service for the church.

Selected Texts:
Clarifying Subjectivity and Limitations

Identifying authors and selecting texts for an anthology is always a subjective endeavor. Here are the parameters used in selecting the works for this book:

- Seminal works that made a significant impact on the field of evangelical Christian education is the priority of this book. There are unquestionably a larger number of respected Christian education scholars who are not identified in this book, many of whom have made significant contributions, and whose names deserve to be recognized. However, this author selected the primary sources he believes have made the most impact across the evangelical Christian education spectrum.

Preface

- Again admittedly subjective, this author selected those chapters from the respective works which he believes are most significant, and presumably helpful to the reader in better understanding the nature of the work.
- While not an exhaustive list, the scholars identified reflect the leading representatives of evangelical Christian education in the mid-twentieth century.
- Lectures delivered or journal articles written by religious educators were not selected. Only books were identified, and chapters from these books were selected.
- Only Christian educators were selected. In addition to theology, Christian educators had become interdisciplinary in their thinking and were greatly informed by other fields, such as psychology, sociology, evolutionary biology, and political science. While many influential theorists no doubt influenced religious education, they were not selected for this book.

Acknowledgments

As always, I begin my acknowledgments with Dr. Gloria Durka, my doctoral advisor. I am also grateful to the faculty at Fordham University's Graduate School of Religion and Religious Education, especially Dr. John Elias, Dr. Harold Horell, and Dr. Kieran Scott.

To Bonita D'Amil, who served as permissions editor. Without her diligence, organization, and expertise in acquiring all the rights of the selected works, this book could not have been published.

Special thanks to Dr. Kevin E. Lawson for his generous foreword, and also for his work on the Christian Educators of the 20th Century Project. This site gathers information on influential Protestant, Orthodox, and Roman Catholic Christian/religious education leaders of the twentieth century. It served as a primary resource for this book, and I use it liberally. Dr. Lawson was also immensely helpful in assisting me in obtaining all the necessary permissions to use the pictures of the featured religious educators. It is with great enthusiasm that I endorse the Christian Educators of the 20th Century Project. For a more comprehensive examination of religious educators identified in this book, and many others, please visit: http://www2.talbot.edu/ce20/.

To the staff of the Starbucks in Nyack, New York, who allowed to work undisturbed for days and hours on end on this book. To the Village of Nyack Library, for providing a wonderful space for me to research and write.

To my mother, Aida, and my sister, Rebecca, for their affirmations. To my wife, Jill, for her continued support and patience with me, my work, and my research, and for listening to my endless monologues on life and religion.

Acknowledgments

As always, I end my acknowledgements with my daughter, Nicole. What a wonderful thing to speak deeply, to reason passionately, to laugh heartily with one's daughter.

Permissions

The author and publisher gratefully acknowledge the permission granted to reproduce the copyrighted material used in this book. Every effort has been made to obtain permission to reproduce copyrighted material from the respective copyright holders. U.S. copyright law allows for use of copyrighted material without permission if all available avenues have been taken to secure permission. The author and publisher apologize for any errors or omissions in the list below and would be grateful if notified of any corrections that should be incorporated in future reprints or editions of this book.

Charles B. Eavey, "The Christian Teacher Preparing to Teach," chapter 5 in *Principles of Teaching for Christian Teachers* (Grand Rapids: Zondervan, 1940).

Findley B. Edge, "Securing Carry-Over," chapter 5 in *Teaching for Results* (Nashville: Broadman, 1956). Copyright © 1956 B&H Publishing Group. Reprinted by permission.

Frank E. Gaebelein, "Preface to Christian Education," in *Christian Education in a Democracy: The Report of the N.A.E. Committee* (Oxford: Oxford University Press, 1951). Reprinted by permission of the National Association of Evangelicals.

Lawrence O. Richards, "The Pattern: HBLT Approach," chapter 9 in *Creative Bible Teaching*, rev. ed., by Lawrence O. Richards and Gary Bredfeldt (Chicago: Moody, 1998). Reprinted by permission.

Permissions

Lois E. LeBar, "Structuring the Curriculum," chapter 8 in *Education That Is Christian* (Westwood, NJ: Revell, 1958).

Permission granted to publish facsimile reproductions of all headshot images of authors, except for Fernando Arzola Jr., from Christian Educators of the 20th Century Project (www.christianeducators20.com), Talbot School of Theology, Biola University.

1

Charles B. Eavey

Principles of Teaching for Christian Teachers (1940)

Regardless of how good a teacher may be, he is not prepared to teach a class until he knows the members of that class. He cannot study the lesson properly or decide intelligently upon his aims and the methods he should use unless he knows whom he is to teach the truth of that lesson.

About Charles B. Eavey

Charles Benton Eavey (1889–1974) was born in Hagerstown, Maryland. He was raised in a family environment that didn't nurture religious affections; however, he later joined the Brethren in Christ. After his non-supportive father died, Eavey dropped out of school at the age of eighteen and worked on the farm in Kansas taking care of his mother and siblings. He returned to school at the age of twenty-one. Eventually, he obtained his PhD from New York University. He taught at Messiah College (1922–1928) and Wheaton College (1930–1942). Eavey established the undergraduate major in Christian education, and laid the foundations for what would later become a Masters in Christian education.[1]

Unfortunately, Eavey was not granted tenure at Wheaton due to various reasons, not the least of which was his confrontational style. He worked odd jobs before securing a position in the personnel department of a Chicago-based corporation. Eavey took this "opportunity" to reorganize his teaching notes into books, of which more than a dozen were published.[2]

About Principles of Teaching for Christian Teachers

His first and most widely read book, *Principles of Teaching for Christian Teachers* enjoyed over twenty printings. Thoroughly evangelical, it also utilized insights from the social sciences.[3]

This is highlighted by the Robert Lay as he writes, "Eavey was both progressive (as his education shows) and evangelical—nurtured in the theologically conservative Brethren in Christ Church and shaped by the evangelistic revivals of the 1910's and 1920's."[4]

Principles of Teaching for Christian Teachers is a dense and technical work. It is both philosophical and methodological. Much of the insight is common knowledge today; however, as a work published in 1940, its popularity is understandable, and one can see how it laid

---

1. Lay, "Charles B. Eavey."
2. Ibid.
3. Burgess, *Models of Religious Education*, 153.
4. Lay, "Charles B. Eavey."

the foundation for many of the future teaching methods books, particularly within evangelical Christian education.

Selected Text:
"The Christian Teacher Preparing to Teach"[5]

The first task of this treatise was to present certain principles that must be considered basic in all Christian teaching; next, the importance of and the necessity for Christian teaching were stressed; then, the aims of the Christian teacher were discussed. In the previous chapter, consideration was given to the subject of what the Christian teacher should be, especially as a person. The task now at hand is to advance some thoughts on the subject of the teacher's preparation for teaching. In a sense this represents a continuation of the subject because development of good teaching personality is one of the most important forms of preparation that can be made for Christian teaching.

But there are other forms of preparation that he who would teach effectively must undergo. Emphasis has been placed on the fact that the teaching process is a twofold one, including both learning and teaching. It has also been seen that whenever teaching is done, there is a person who is to learn, a person who is to stimulate, guide, and direct the learning, and a content to be learned. It would seem to be obvious, then, that the effective teacher would need to know the one taught, what to teach him, and how to teach. And logically it would seem also that to teach aright one would need to know the school in which he is teaching.

This gives knowledge as one essential for good teaching. An art as intricate as teaching can be learned best by observing how others do it; hence observation is a second essential. And without practice, one could scarcely hope to attain any high degree of success no matter how much he may know or how much he may observe; therefore, doing becomes a third essential. The effective teacher must know, observe, and do.[6] Obviously, preparation for teaching is important, as is also the means available for the training of teachers. The subjects

---

5. Ch. 5 in Eavey, *Principles of Teaching for Christian Teachers*.
6. Raffety, *Smaller Sunday School Makes Good*, 154.

that will be discussed in the present chapter are, then: (1) the need for teacher preparation; (2) learning to know: (a) the pupil; (b) subject matter; (c) how to teach; (d) the school; (3) observing as preparation for teaching; (4) doing in preparation for teaching; (5) means available for teacher preparation.

1. The Need for Teacher Preparation

The teacher is the all important factor in any school. Quite evidently, every single thing that has any bearing upon the pupils in a school affects the quality of the teaching. Thus, the type of building, the equipment and materials, the organization and administration of the school, the conditions of home life, the ideals of the community, and everything else that affects the life of the pupil exerts influence on the teaching of Christian truth in the church school.

The teacher is the most important factor in a school. But the factor that looms highest in importance is the teacher. Of what avail is it if the school is housed in the finest building equipped with the best in material things if the teaching is not done well? Of what worth is a good curriculum and expert administration if the teacher in the classroom does not know how to teach? What can ideal home life and good public sentiment accomplish, so far as the work of a school is concerned, if the teacher in that school is so poorly prepared that he cannot teach efficiently? In fact, poor work in the classroom, as was pointed out in an earlier chapter, can do much to inculcate wrong habits and attitudes in children. On the other hand, one truly and fully prepared to teach may do very effective work without the aid of these external advantages, valuable as these may be for the accomplishment of worthwhile results.

Teacher training is necessary. Effectiveness in teaching depends largely upon the adequacy of preparation. Well-trained teachers make good schools where pupils learn what they are taught. But if preparation has been superficial, haphazard, or misdirected, pupils cannot learn well, if at all. This fact is recognized in secular education. No public-school teacher can come to his task without specific preparation for the particular work he is to do. Then he does his teaching in buildings designed for educational purposes with all the equipment and materials necessary for effective accomplishment. And the public-school teacher works under conditions intended to make for definite improvement in teaching.

Training of Christian teachers must be adequate. Why should children of today be denied the right to as much opportunity to learn Bible truth as they have to learn history, science, arithmetic, and the other subjects commonly taught in the public school? And if children have a right to Bible knowledge, do they not have the further right to efficient teaching of the Bible? Is it true that just anyone, whether he has had training or not, is sufficient for impartation of knowledge of the Bible while only the highly trained are permitted to teach secular subjects? Does the putting of names such as "Sunday," "Sabbath," "Bible," or "Church" in front of the word "school" mean that some mystical occurrence will make it unnecessary for the teachers in that school to be prepared? Certainly any person who is at all interested in the highest welfare of children and who has any conception of relative values and eternal verities would not hesitate for a moment to say, "It is the right of every child to have teachers of Bible who can present the Word in the most effective manner."

The Christian teacher of today unprepared for his specific work is at a tremendous disadvantage, and his being at a disadvantage reflects discredit not only upon him but upon the cause for which he stands. How can a boy or a girl who attends public school five days a week where he gets the very best instruction from a well trained teacher have much respect for an unprepared or a poorly prepared Sunday-school teacher under whom he or she sits for an hour of undirected or misdirected activity on Sunday? How much value is such a boy or a girl likely to attach to that which the Sunday-school teacher is supposed to be teaching? And how much respect can he or she have for a church that perpetrates upon him the outrage, having the audacity to call the work "Christian education"? Any normal boy or girl makes the comparison between the work done in the public school and that done in the church school as inevitably as he would make the comparison between riding behind an ox-team and riding in the latest model of automobile, were he required to use the former means of transportation in this modern age. That the comparison is less striking because it is perhaps less conscious does not make the attitude formed without the most untoward results

Evangelical Christian Education

Dr. Walter S. Athearn has spoken words in this connection the truth of which may well be pondered and weighed by all:

> Society protects its *land* from the ravishes of unskilled tenants; it insists that justice be not thwarted by untrained jurists; it guards the bodies of its citizenship from the untrained "quack"; it excludes the charlatan from the schoolroom that the *minds* of our children may not be maimed and crippled by unskilled workmen; but the souls of children have been left unprotected from malpractice at the hands of well-meaning, but untrained workers in the field of religious education.
>
> It is strange that the last resource that society has attempted to conserve is the spiritual life of the children. It is just now beginning to dawn upon Christian people that there is such a thing as *spiritual malpractice,* and that the pious, well-meaning church-school teacher may ignorantly pull up by the roots and destroy the very elements which enable the soul to bring forth the fruits of the Spirit....
>
> We give all honor to the faithful men and women of the past who gave of their best to the cause they loved more than life itself; but a new day has come, and new demands must be made of those who serve in the Lord's House. To sincerity, devotion, noble Christian character, we must add that technical skill which comes from instruction and training.

Obligations for obtaining thorough preparation. The conscientious Christian teacher will, therefore, feel very keenly the obligation to God, first of all, for the specific command is, "Study to shew thyself approved unto God." He will feel it is an obligation to his pupils also because, as a Christian teacher, he has responsibility for their spiritual and eternal welfare. One unguided, careless, or superficial act of a single teacher may determine the unhappy future destiny of a pupil or of pupils. Finally, the teacher will feel that he owes it to himself to prepare in the best possible manner for his great task. Teaching, like all other work, yields its greatest rewards to those who take its responsibilities most seriously and who make most diligent effort to fit themselves to do the work well. Consequently, the teacher who is willing to pay the price of hard study, increasing devotion, and holding a fixed determination to master a difficult art is the one who will realize greatest satisfaction from his teaching. Such an one will find himself "a workman that needeth not to be ashamed."

2. The Knowledge Needed for Adequate Preparation

As was mentioned, knowledge is one essential to preparation for good teaching. It is fundamental to the other two essentials, for one must know before he can observe intelligently or do effectively. Also the more completely, accurately, and fully one knows, the better he can observe and do. To be well-prepared, the teacher should aim at the mastery of four kinds of knowledge: (a) knowledge of pupils; (b) knowledge of content to be taught; (c) knowledge of the technique of teaching; (d) knowledge of the school in which the teaching is done.

a) The Teacher Learning to Know His Pupils

Regardless of how good a teacher may be, he is not prepared to teach a class until he knows the members of that class. He cannot study the lesson properly or decide intelligently upon his aims and the methods he should use unless he knows whom he is to teach the truth of that lesson. Nor is it sufficient that the teacher study the class or the children in general; he must know the individual boy or girl whom he is to teach. Of course, these two kinds of knowledge overlap somewhat: the better a teacher knows children the more easily he can understand a child, and as he learns to know the individual child, he gains better understanding of children in general.

Specific study of pupil traits. Before the teacher begins to teach, therefore, he should learn all that he can about his pupils. He should understand their nature and needs in their particular stage of development; he should know their capacities and attainments, their interests and their normal experiences, their attitudes and their modes of thought, their problems and their difficulties. If he is teaching primary children, he will need to make a particular study of children of that age; if he is teaching young people, he will need to learn all that he can about young people. In other words, specific study of the characteristics of the particular age level being taught is an essential preparation for good teaching.

Study of physical life. Upon this study as a foundation, the effective Christian teacher will find himself able to make particular study of the pupils in his class. To understand them aright, he must know something about their heredity and environment. He should understand that the influences of environment are being exerted continually, modifying what the child received from heredity. He will study the physical characteristics of each pupil, learning his rate of physical growth and observing the factors that influence growth and physical development. He will ascertain whether or not he has defects that will mitigate against effective learning and he will gain appreciation of the particular conditions that affect the physical life of the individual pupil.

Mental, social, and personal life. The thorough-going teacher will also study the mental life of each pupil to learn his level of mental ability, the kinds of reaction and the modes of response that are peculiar to him, and the outlook he has as a consequence of his type of mental life. He will acquaint himself with the major interests, physical, mental, spiritual, and social, of each pupil. He will learn something about his companions, his recreations, his home life, and his religious views. He will also be concerned about and, interested in the problems and difficulties of each pupil. His careful, persistent, individual study will enable him not only to detect these but to be quick to bring to bear the emphasis necessary for correct solution of problems and adequate meeting of difficulties.

Recognition of individual differences. An alert teacher will recognize individual differences among his pupils. A principal of a school once said that if he had a class of fifty scholars, he would try to be fifty different teachers, as he turned from one to another of those scholars to instruct them. A very successful teacher of boys maintained that his practice was to teach only one boy at a time; he left to one side, as it were, all the other pupils in the class while he centered his attention upon one. These teachers were doing what every teacher must do—teaching individuals. There is no other way to teach; pupils never learn as a class. No teacher can teach intelligently until he knows the ways in which each pupil is different from every other.

Charles B. Eavey

It is utterly impossible to make wise adaptation of either subject matter or technique unless the teacher understands the peculiarities of each pupil. If a pupil is tender and loving, appeal must be made to him in a way different than would be used with a pupil of cool, calculating disposition. One pupil likes to delve into the depths of abstruse thought; another delights in stories and illustrations that require little thinking on his part. One lives in his feelings; another reasons out everything. This pupil is living in conscious fellowship and communion with God; that one is harassed by doubts and fears. Each has his individuality, and the teacher must understand his ways of reacting before he can hope to be of any service to him.

Knowing the language of pupils. To teach aright, the teacher and the pupil must speak a common language.[7]

In other words, the teacher must be able so to speak that the pupil understands what he says. The greater the difference between the ages of the teacher and the pupils the more likely is the former to use language which the latter does not comprehend. As one becomes well acquainted with a field or subject and the words in it, he is quite likely to assume that others are as well acquainted with either or both as he himself is. For example, a mature, enthusiastic, devoted Christian teacher might use terms such as "knowing the Lord," "being saved," "the coming of the Lord," etc., the meaning of which his pupils who are unfamiliar with Christian and Biblical terminology could not grasp without explanation. To the end that the language used in teaching may be common to teacher and pupil, the teacher need study constantly and carefully the conversation of the pupils so that he may express himself as far as possible in terms that are comprehensible to them.

In addition to making unwarranted assumptions about the language understood by pupils, the teacher may assume too much concerning the state of the child's knowledge. The teacher of the man who was surprised to learn that "Dan and Beersheba were places" because he always thought "they were husband and wife like Sodom and Gomorrah" would be quite ineffective in teaching him facts of the Old Testament geography so long as he thus thought. Perhaps it was Coleridge who said, "We cannot make another comprehend our

7. Trumbull, *Teaching and Teachers*, 38.

knowledge, until we first know his ignorance." So long as a teacher assumes that a pupil knows what he does not know, he will be severely handicapped in teaching him in that connection. The prepared teacher knows the attainments, general and specific, of each of his pupils and thus is able to bring to them new knowledge in terms of what they already know.

b) The Teacher Learning to Know His Subject Matter

When the teacher knows the pupil, his nature, needs, interests, characteristics, attainments, etc., there comes the question: What shall I teach him? In seeking to answer this question, it must be kept in mind very definitely that what a pupil is taught is never an end in itself. Not what he knows but what he is as a result of coming to know is the acid test of teaching. The teacher uses subject matter as a means to the end of bringing about results in the life of the pupil. In terms of our aims, it may be said that Christian teaching uses the content for the purpose of bringing the pupil to Christ, building him up in Christ, and sending him out for Christ. So the test of the effectiveness of the Christian teacher's work is not how much the pupils know about the Bible and related subjects but how fully the knowledge of these becomes effective in the lives of the pupils.

The Bible the subject matter of the Christian teacher. The last sentence suggests what the subject matter of the Christian teacher is: "the Bible and related subjects." The Bible is the revealed Word of God given to man that he may know whence he comes and whither he goes, that he may be perfected for the eternal destiny which a loving God intended for him, and that he may be completely furnished for living the life which God wishes him to live. The Bible, therefore, is basic content for Christian teaching, and it is not the Bible as a book, nor as a piece of historical literature, nor as a presentation of social Christianity that is basic; it is the Bible as God's Word, as the Word of life. What the truly Christian teacher finds in the Bible "is not merely a record, or a series of documents, or a depository of truth, nor a treasure house of fine art and good morals, but God's powerful living Word, which enters the soul, to bring it to repentance and faith, to transform it and to build it into Christ."

Charles B. Eavey

"Related subjects" comprise things the teacher needs to know in order to make the Bible message clearly understood. In addition to a thorough knowledge of the textbook, the teacher should be familiar with the geography of Bible lands, ancient history, antiquities and customs of Bible lands, and missionary principles and progress. Other fields of knowledge which may well form part of the equipment of the most thorough-going teacher are: knowledge of church history, especially the history of his own church, understanding of the principle doctrinal tenets of his church, familiarity with the great social and political movements of the day, and current events of every-day life. Acquaintances with great masterpieces of literature, music, and art will also be found very helpful.

The teacher's two kinds of study. In learning to know subject matter, the study of the teacher will assume two forms: (1) general, directed toward making himself complete and well-rounded in his knowledge of what he is to teach; (2) special, directed toward thorough preparation of the particular lesson. Since the material in bulk for the Christian teacher is his Bible and since he must know it better than any other book, the remainder of the treatment of this topic will be devoted to consideration of how the teacher should study his Bible.

(1) The teacher learning to know the Bible. The effective teacher is always a student of that which he is teaching. To teach intelligently and practically any portion of the subject, he must be familiar with the whole. Without thorough understanding of the whole subject, the material to be taught cannot be organized and used to meet the needs of the pupils. No matter what the subject is, the teacher must be engaged continually in study, keeping fresh his gained store of knowledge and ever expanding in his field. This is the price he must pay in order to be a good teacher.

What real study is. Every teacher needs, therefore, to understand the meaning and purpose of study and to stimulate himself to the love of study, investigation, research, and problem-solving. "*All real study involves investigative thinking*—problem solving, mental exploration, a quest for truth. Letting the thoughts of another pass uncritically through one's mind, meditating upon what one already knows, memorizing what someone else has said, may be valuable aids to study, but they are not essentially study. Study, in the true sense of the word, occurs only when the mind is confronted with a difficulty, a problem, a novel situation. The initial step in the process of study is to recognize the difficulty and proceed to define it; after which possibilities of solution are suggested by reasoning based on experience—one's own and that of the race; conclusions thus reached to be carefully checked by observation and verification."[8]

Some practical suggestions for one who wishes to stimulate himself along the lines of effective study are: maintain a good physical condition; provide conditions favorable to study such as light, temperature, ventilation, absence of distractions, etc.; have a regular time and place to study; form systematic habits in study; maintain an attitude of interest and attention; determine the purpose of study; assume a problem solving attitude; make careful notes and outlines; and have a sufficient motive for study.

Why the Christian teacher studies the Bible. The motive of the Christian teacher in studying the Bible is to gain thorough knowledge of the whole Bible—not knowledge which will make him a Bible scholar but such knowledge as will enable him to interpret the truths aright to the minds and hearts of his pupils. His aim is to get a reasonable understanding of its contents, not necessarily an exegetical understanding. Although detailed knowledge may be most helpful, it is not necessary to master the technicalities to gain a working knowledge of the Bible. No one can teach a portion of the Bible to advantage until he has a knowledge of the sixty-six books. Without a comprehensive understanding of the whole, preparation for the teaching of separate lessons becomes most burdensome and ultimately fruitless. The teacher, therefore, must study the Bible as a book, not in little, isolated fragments.

Conditions of effective Bible study. There are certain fundamental conditions for most profitable Bible study. Anyone who meets these conditions will get more out of the Bible while pursuing the poorest method of study than will the one who does not meet them even if he uses the best method of study. First, he who would really know the Bible must be born again. The natural man receives not the things of the Spirit; one must have spiritual perception to be an understanding student and a competent teacher of the Bible. Second,

---

8. Dobbins, *How to Teach Young People and Adults*, 64

to know the Bible one must have love for the Bible. It must be studied with real appetite, not from a mere sense of duty. Third, he who would know the Bible must be willing to do hard work. Its hidden treasures cannot be found without digging. Study means the putting forth of diligent effort. Fourth, the student of the Bible must have a will absolutely surrendered to God. Without such surrender, he will lack that clearness of vision and that teachableness of heart necessary for the revelation of truth by the Holy Spirit and no one can understand the Bible without this revelation. Fifth, he must be obedient to revealed light. "Be ye doers of the Word and not hearers only." Every duty which one fails to perform obscures some truth he should know. Sixth, a child-like mind and spirit are essential. Simple, trusting faith, meek teachableness of spirit, and unbiased acceptance of the truth must characterize him who would know the Bible. Seventh, it must be studied as the Word of God. This involves unquestioning acceptance of its teachings, absolute reliance upon its promises, and wholehearted obedience to its commands. The Bible is not a book of magic but a revelation of the will of God. Eighth, the Bible must be studied in the spirit of prayer. Simple, trustful looking to God, asking Him to reveal. His meaning, must accompany intellectual effort on the part of him who sincerely desires to know its message.

For the general mastery of the Bible as a whole, several fruitful forms of study may be used. The Christian teacher who is desirous of attaining to the best working mastery of its content will find it worth while to study in all these ways at one time or another. However, each individual may wish to follow predominately that particular method of study toward which his personal disposition and past experience incline him most favorably.

The synthetic method of Bible study. By beginning at Genesis and going on to Revelation, one gets a view of the Bible as a whole. Such a mode of study gives unity, helping to prevent one-sidedness and partial views of the truth. It also makes for a perspective in which overemphasis on particular teachings and portions have no place. To avoid the tendency to monotony and consequent lack of interest due to the reading and study of the same type of content too long at a time, the user of this method can study the Old Testament and the New at the same time. One can read the Bible through in a year by reading six chapters daily. A simple plan is to read two chapters daily from each of three portions: the Old Testament, beginning with Genesis, the portion beginning with Psalms, and the New Testament.

The study of the Bible by individual books. This is a very good method. The beginner should choose a short book, one that is comparatively easy and one that is especially rich in content. The first step in such study is to master the general content of the book. Reading it through at one sitting without stopping to deal with difficulties is a good way to begin. A certain preacher who used this method of study very effectively said that he read a book through one hundred times as a preliminary to intensive study. Preparation of an introduction to the book, the making of an outline of the book, and the marking of the great passages are further steps. Finally, each verse should be studied and pondered, the results of the whole study classified, and the findings of the process meditated upon and digested. Bible study of this kind is very rich and satisfying to both mind and heart.

The study of the Bible by topics. This is a very systematic, thorough, and exact method. Topics such as "God," "faith," "salvation," "prayer," "Christ," "The Holy Spirit," and the like, studied with the aid of a good concordance or even with the aid of a reference Bible constitutes an interesting and very profitable exercise. One of the helps often found in Bibles is a subject-index, in which the references to many of the great subjects treated in the Bible are presented in outline form. With the aid of such an outline, a student may make an intensive study of important topics.

Biographical study of the Bible. To use this method the student selects one great character after another, collects all passages dealing with the person studied, and analyzes his character. Strong and weak points should be noted, and the lessons can be summarized. Thus glimpses of God's ways in dealing with men and men's wrong and right attitudes toward God can be learned. All of the lessons can then be applied in the teacher's own spiritual development as well as to the lives of the pupils. This is an interesting method and one which yields very worth while results.

The study of the Bible by types. By use of this method the student can gain good understanding of the message of the Bible. The Old Testament sets forth in shadow and figure the reality which the New presents. The law had a "shadow of good things to come and not the very image of the things" (Heb. 10:1). To study by types necessitates looking up all Scripture references dealing with that which is being studied and getting full meaning of names and places under consideration. One who uses this method must ever be on guard against the fanciful and the making of interpretations not warranted by the Scriptures. Rightly and carefully used, the method can be most helpful in getting an accurate understanding of the teachings of Scripture.

The study of the Bible for practical usefulness. This method yields rich returns. The Bible was not written to be used as a book of culture but as a book of spiritual guidance. To study it for practical purposes gives the student a vision of how perfectly it is adapted to man's need. The teacher who uses this method of study will catch constantly new meaning of the Bible in relation to the needs of men—his own as well as others. In seeking food for others he himself will be fed. Whatever the problem, difficulty, burden, or perplexity that confronts one, the Bible has a message that throws light upon it and gives safety and comfort.

(2) The teacher learning to know the lesson. Knowledge of the pupils to be taught and general knowledge of the Bible to be taught these pupils are two things the teacher must know. Next comes a knowledge of the special truth to be taught. The study of a lesson in preparation for its teaching is an art that should be mastered thoroughly by every Christian teacher. However well a teacher may know his Bible and however long he may have taught, the diligent preparation of each lesson is a necessity for most effective teaching. Marion Lawrance said, "The greatest need in our church work today is trained teachers who will put their whole mind into their preparation, their whole soul into their presentation, and their whole life into their illustration." No teacher who values success or who has a sense of responsibility for his pupils will enter a classroom to teach, relying on his general knowledge of content or depending on a few minutes of hurried preparation for the teaching of the lesson.

The materials for study. An important factor in the preparation of a lesson is the source of the materials. Obviously, since the Bible is the textbook of the Christian school, it should be the teacher's first study. While good lesson helps may be a valuable aid, a teacher should not depend on these primarily. Lesson helps should be used with the Bible and never apart from it. Furthermore, helps should be used for the purpose of getting light on the meaning of the Bible text. A true teacher will study the Bible text and the Bible context before he uses helps, for he knows that the Bible is its own best interpreter. The best way to get light on obscure passages is to compare Scripture with Scripture.

In this connection, it may be well to recognize that there are various kinds of Bibles. For instance, there is the Bible that has in the back many valuable, historical, geographical, encyclopedic, and other kinds of helps. Some of these have considerable value but most of that which is given can be found in other volumes. Then there are Bibles that have notes and comments on various passages; in other words, a sort of commentary on the text is provided. While such explanations are valuable for certain purposes, especially to a beginner, they have the effect of discouraging independent thinking, for the natural tendency of the student is to accept the opinion of the commentator as his own without having investigated its foundation. The best kind of Bible for the teacher to use is a good chain-reference Bible so that parallel passages may be independently investigated and passage compared with passage. One great thing the teacher should do for his pupils is to make them independent investigators of truth and this he cannot do unless he himself is an investigator. One form of help the teacher's study Bible should have is good maps.

Other sources of material the teacher should have are: an English dictionary; a good Bible dictionary; a concordance such as Strong's, Young's or Cruden's complete concordance. A good Bible commentary may well be used for the purpose of ascertaining what interpretations and explanations have been given difficult passages by Bible scholars. Gray's *Christian Workers' Commentary* is a good one-volume work. A complete set of Jamieson, Fausset, and Brown is recommended for those who desire a more exhaustive commentary.

The plan of study. A second important factor in the teacher's preparation of a lesson is a plan of study. To be successful, study must be pursued according to a system. The spending of much time is to no avail if the teacher is not prepared to teach after he has spent the time. He will not be well prepared if his study lacks a plan. So each teacher should formulate and follow a plan such as will enable him to accomplish the best results of which he is capable. No plan is alike desirable for and helpful to all teachers.

Charles B. Eavey

In studying the lessons from the Bible, the teacher will, first of all, need to get an understanding of the words. Then he will find it necessary to ascertain their connected meanings. Next he will wish to make practical applications of these meanings. In other words, the first thing is the simple text of the lesson, the second is the plan for teaching of the text, and the last is the application of truths taught. The teacher wants to know what is said, what is meant by what is said, and what the bearing of all this is on his pupils.

Studying in terms of pupil needs. As he studies, the teacher does well to keep in mind the individual members of his class. His constant study of individual pupils and their needs will reveal ways in which help may be given under the guidance of the Holy Spirit. Then he will look for and recognize in the lesson those special portions that should be chosen for each of the pupils. This will be true not only of instruction that may be imparted but also of guidance of pupils in their personal research or direction of them in their work. In all his study, the Christian teacher will be tapping reservoirs that enrich his own life. Like Chaucer's pastor, he will be teaching others in the way he himself has first followed.

Knowing more than can be taught. A warning that may well be sounded for the benefit of a hard working teacher is that there is much more in every lesson than he can hope to teach. One who has made most thorough preparation sometimes becomes discouraged when he finds that time is too short to present all his gathered material. It is a poor teacher who teaches on the fringe of what he knows; everyone should know much more than he can present. Goethe says, "Nothing is worse than a teacher who knows only as much as he has to make known to the scholar." For the work of true teaching it is not so much a question of how much the teacher knows about the lesson as it is of how much change he is able to bring about in the pupils. If he knows a great deal more than he can teach, the teacher can select here and there from his stores to suit the needs of those taught. Not what the teacher could teach but what has happened to the pupil because the teacher has taught is the test of the worth of the teaching.

Dependence on prayer. Finally, it may be said that all the study of the Christian teacher is done in dependence upon the power and guidance of the Holy Spirit. In prayer, he approaches the lesson, through prayer he obtains understanding of the lesson, and by means of prayer he brings the lesson to bear on the lives of his pupils. Fervent prayer helps him over the greatest obstacles, and with prayer he conquers for Christ. Whatever he may have by way of training and whatever he does by way of effort in study are only instrumental forces which, taken and used by God, bring to pass spiritual results in the lives of pupils. Christian teaching is not done in the power and strength of human effort.

c) Knowledge of How to Teach

One may know his pupils, one may know his Bible, and be well prepared in knowledge of the lesson and yet be unable to teach effectively. Everything that is done must be done by some method. Both experience and observation teach that there are some ways of doing things that are more effective than others, therein be no teaching without some kind of method. As in everything else, so in teaching, he who knows how to do will get best results. The fact that the work being done is Christian teaching does not make it any less important that he who does it should know how to do No one is ready to teach until he knows what to teach, but, in addition, he must also know how to teach.

Knowledge of a subject is one thing, but ability to make that knowledge available practically and effectively to others is quite another thing. Who would want to be treated for some physical ailment by a doctor who knew much about medical science if he was not able to reduce what he knew to practice in treating a particular case? Of what worth to a person who wants a house would an architect or a contractor be if he knew all about the different styles of architecture but could not arrange the building material so that part fitted to part? Likewise, the teacher who knows his pupils ever so well and who has thorough master, of what he would teach is not prepared for his work, unless he can effect changes in the lives of those pupils through the right use of what he knows about his subject. So far as any Christian teacher is concerned, the Bible will be a dead book to his pupils until he is able to make it live in their lives.

All teaching is done by some method. All teachers use some method of teaching. The method used mar be faulty, careless, ineffective, even weak or harmful, or it may be strong and very effective. To succeed it, his work, any teacher must have understanding of the way in which learning takes place, and with this as a basis, he must use ways of organizing, presenting, and handling content, materials, and activities to meet pupils' needs, interests, and abilities. The Christian teacher trained and consecrated to his work will need to guard against two dangers; careless, haphazard method or such dependence on method as will hinder the Holy Spirit in His operation. There need be no conflict between careful, well planned teacher activity and the work of the Holy Spirit. On the contrary, it is reasonable to think that the Holy Spirit can use a teacher better in choosing a proper method and good plans than He can use a teacher who attempts to teach a class without preparing carefully and intelligently to do so.

Principles and method. There are various methods of teaching, and no two teaching situations are ever exactly alike. More accurately, it may be said that there is no set "method" of teaching, but a variety of "methods" basic to which are certain principles of teaching that must be mastered by him who would be successful. Then, when he teaches, he will make use of this, that, or the other mode of procedure as may be best for achieving the objective in mind. Not all lessons can be taught in the same way. One pupil will have to be handled this way and another in some other way to accomplish the same results. One teacher can use most successfully a technique which, used by a fellow teacher, would result in dismal failure. For the achievement of a certain aim, it may be advisable to use one method while the attainment of another outcome may necessitate the employment of a very different method. Factors such as the age and the maturity of the pupils, the attitudes and interests of the class, the physical equipment and facilities, and the materials for study will also have a part in determining what is the best way for the teacher to present the materials of instruction.

But, let it be reiterated, in order to make this choice, the teacher must know the principles basic to good teaching. What are these principles? They have been stated in various ways by many writers, but it seems that the following seven principles should be studied by any teacher who wishes to know how to teach. Some of these have been dealt with earlier in this treatise and some will receive consideration in later pages. Briefly stated, they are:

There is no teaching without learning. Consequently, the teacher must know how

learning takes place and how to direct the activities of pupils so that desired growth and adjustment result. What is learned by the pupils is a test of the effectiveness of the technique used.

The pupil does the learning. All learning comes throng self-activity. No amount of teacher-activity in and of itself produces learning. Telling is not teaching; lecturing is not teaching; doing is not teaching. Only as the teacher gets reaction of individuals to certain items in the total situation will pupils learn and be able to recall those things.

The motivation of the pupil determines what he will learn. Interest must be sought and maintained; attention must be won and held. The learning activities of pupils should be adequately motivated and guided toward definitely conceived learning outcomes.

The mental set of a learner at a particular moment is most potent in determining the nature of the learning response. The teacher should do everything within his power to secure the most favorable conditions. physical, mental, and emotional.

Various ways of learning make variety in teaching necessary. The intelligent teacher, far from becoming enamored with any formal mode of procedure, will be concerned primarily with the problem of how to get the work done rather than with what kind of tools to use. Tools, like subject matter, are a means to an end.

The teacher needs to plan most carefully and thorough, for the teaching of each separate lesson. The objectives need to be very clearly perceived, the subject matter arranged in terms of the steps taken in learning, and provision made for every step in the learning process.

Every teacher should be improving his method constantly. He needs to be analyzing the total process of teaching and rating himself without ceasing. He should maintain an alert, experimental attitude in all teaching situations. Without self-criticism there can be no growth, and a teacher who is not growing is a poor teacher.

d) Knowing the School

To be most effective, the teacher needs an understanding of the school in which he teaches. Any school is an organization. To fill his place properly, a person who is part of an organization must know something about the manner in which that organization functions. A church school exists for the purpose of making Christian teaching possible. Instructing and training pupils in the things of God to the end that they become mature Christians is the function of the church school. It must therefore be a *school*. It must be administered like a school. Each member of the organization has certain responsibilities for the work of the whole, and each should know and keep his place.

The teacher stands central in any school, for no matter how large or how well organized a school may be, it is the work of the teacher in the classroom that determines whether or not the function of the school is being fulfilled. If the teacher fails, the school fails. Regardless of outward show, a school is only as good as the teaching done in it. Good teachers make good schools. The position of teacher is, therefore, the most important position in the school.

But the church school must be administered with proper responsibility all along the line from pupil to teacher, from teacher to superintendent, from superintendent to minister. The superintendent should realize that his major charge is to protect and promote the teaching ministry. The teacher should understand what his responsibility is to the other members of the organization so that he can work harmoniously with all for the accomplishment of the great purpose for which the school exists. Only as each person in the church school discharges effectively the task that is his to do can the work of the whole go forward to successful conclusion.

3. Observation as Preparation for Teaching

Mere knowledge acquirement, however complete and thorough it be, is inadequate for fullness of preparation for teaching. In the performance of any kind of activity, one should be guided by a model, or mental pattern, representing what he is trying to do. For the Christian teacher, the best means of acquiring such a pattern is through observing teaching. Keen observation of the good teaching of public-school teachers of children of the same age as those whom he is teaching and of other teachers in church schools gives him opportunity to study specific teaching situations and to take account of just how particular desired reactions can be secured.

For observation to be most effective, certain conditions should be met. In the first place, the observer should have made sufficient study previously of some phase of the work to be observed to enable him to form intelligent judgment as to the effectiveness of what is seen. Second, the inexperienced observer should limit the number of topics of observation to a few and make preliminary study of the essential features of each. Confusion will result from an attempt to note too many things. Third, the observer should maintain an attitude of open-mindedness with respect to the teaching he sees. There is a very strong tendency for one to be prejudiced greatly in favor of teaching as he was taught. The point of view of the pupil in the class is so different that he cannot gather worthwhile intelligence of what is best in the classroom, particularly as regards instruction. And even if they were completely appraised, methods that are current in the best schools even of the present day may not be so good that they can be safely imitated. The observer should be open minded to the degree that he can see what is actually done and be able to accept or reject in terms of what is commendable or condemnatory in that which is seen.

4. Doing Interpretation for Teaching

No one can develop skill in teaching without practice; one can learn to do only by doing. Mere practice, however, never makes perfect. Unless it is practice of the right procedure, practice will be clumsy, wasteful, and imperfect. If one practices on the basis of accurate knowledge, sound theory, and wide observation, with adequate provision for constant correction and improvement, whenever and wherever these are required, he will improve. Constructive criticism by another, especially if he be experienced in teaching, will be of great value in connection with practice. However, the individual who practices should have the information and know the standards needed for self-criticism. In the last analysis, all criticism must become self-criticism, for only as one accepts the criticism and gives it meaning in the light of standards he apprehends does it become effective for him.

5. Means Available for Teacher Preparation

Where there is a will, there is a way. A teacher who wants to secure good training can secure it somehow, some way. Universities, some colleges, some seminaries, and a few Bible institutes offer courses emphasizing various phases of religious education. To those who cannot avail themselves of the privilege of attendance at such institutions, there are afforded various other opportunities. Conventions and camp conferences often present opportunities for intensive study for ten days or two weeks and sometimes for longer periods. Teacher-training classes can be organized either in the local church or community. Such a class can meet once a week for ten or twelve weeks, two hours a week for five or six weeks, or two hours an evening for five or six evenings in one week. Usually the first of these plans is best.

A teacher or a few teachers who feel the need of training, or a superintendent who first realizes the need, can gather together some interested workers and form a class, select a teacher, and arrange for a time of meeting. With this group as a nucleus other teachers and officers may be drawn into the class. Persons not in active service who give promise of usefulness in the work of Christian teaching may also become interested and thus obtain preparation for future activity. Along with study of the principles of teaching, frequent visits to classes may be made for the purpose of observation. Members of the class who are teaching at present have a chance to test the truths of their lessons and others can occasionally assist, or substitute for an experienced teacher, though inexperienced persons should not be given too heavy responsibilities lest they become discouraged.

Every Sunday school might well have a normal class or a teacher-training class composed of young people in training as prospective teachers. This class could meet during the regular Sunday school hour and take up some definite work that would fit its members for teaching. Thus there would be kept before the minds of youth the possibility of their serving by teaching. From the membership of this class, past and present, recruits may be drawn for the teaching staff of the school as need arises from time to time.

The individual who wishes to prepare to teach or to become effective in teaching, who cannot avail himself of any of these means of preparation, need not despair. For such an one there are good books and departmental magazines. Every teacher should read each year a few books bearing on his teaching field. A magazine offers fresh material from month to month. Another form of training open to the individual teacher is correspondence courses that are offered by many denominations and some colleges and universities. The individual teacher in service can subject himself to continual self-supervision by keeping a record of his work and criticizing himself objectively. Thus he can greatly improve his own teaching.

In short, he who is impressed with a sense of responsibility to God and to others for getting needed preparation will secure it. Such an one will not rob self, nor others who could profit by his expenditure of energy and time, nor be unfair to God whom he serves. The challenge of these words comes to every Christian teacher:

> *There is no chance, no destiny, no fate*
> *Can circumvent, or hinder or control*
> *The firm resolve of a determined soul.*
> *Gifts count for little; will alone is great.*
> *No man can place a limit on thy strength,*
> *All heights are thine, if thou wilt but believe*
> *In thy Creator and thyself. At length*
> *Some feet must tread some heights now unattained.*
> *Why not thine own? Press on. Achieve!*

Questions and Problems

What kinds of preparation should a Christian teacher make for his work?

1. Emphasize the need for preparation on the part of the teacher.

2. Does a Christian teacher need to prepare any less than a teacher in a public school?
3. To whom does the Christian teacher owe obligations?
4. What four kinds of knowledge are essential to adequate preparation for teaching? Which do you think is most important?
5. For what reasons does a teacher need to know his pupils?
6. What should the teacher know about his pupils?
7. Why must the teacher understand individual differences?
8. Can a teacher teach a group or is teaching always an individual matter?
9. Do you think that teachers often assume that their pupils know more than they really do?
10. What is the one test of the effectiveness of teaching?
11. Enumerate things other than the Bible that a Christian needs to know. Why should he know these?
12. Which of the two forms of study of subject matter is more important? Why?
13. What is real study?
14. Name conditions essential to effective study.
15. Enumerate conditions essential to profitable study of the Bible.
16. Comment on each of the methods of Bible study suggested, emphasizing the particular merits.
17. Have you found other methods that are helpful?
18. Outline a good plan for the study of a particular lesson.
19. What materials, other than the Bible, may be used to good advantage in the study of the lesson?
20. Emphasize the importance of the teacher's keeping individual pupils in mind as he studies.
21. What is method?
22. Which is more important for a teacher to know, method or principles? Why?

Evangelical Christian Education

23. Give the essence of the seven principles of teaching.
24. For what reasons is it important that a teacher know the school?
25. State the conditions for most effective observation.
26. How can a teacher use doing as a means of preparation for teaching?
27. What are the means which a teacher can use to secure training?
28. Show the importance of a teacher-training class.

References

Betts, G. H. *Teaching Religion Today.* New York: Abingdon, 1934.
Burton, W. H. *Supervision and the Improvement of Teaching.* New York: Appleton, 1922.
Crawford, C. E. *How to Teach.* Los Angeles: Southern California School Book Depository, 1938.
Dobbins, G. S. *How to Teach Young People and Adults in the Sunday School.* Nashville: Sunday School Board of the Southern Baptist Convention, 1930.
Fergusson, E. M. *Teaching Christianity.* New York: Revell, 1929.
Fiske, G. W. *Purpose in Teaching Religion.* New York: Abingdon, 1927.
Hamer. N. C. *The Educational Work of the Church.* New York: Abingdon, 1939.
Lotz, P. H., and L. W. Crawford. *Studies in Religious Education.* Nashville: Cokesbury, 1931.
McLester, F. C. *Our Pupils and How They Learn.* Nashville: Cokesbury, 1930.
Myers, A. J. W. *Teaching Religion.* Philadelphia: Westminster, 1930.
Plummer, L. F. *The Soul Winning Teacher.* New York: Revell, 1934.
Price, J. M. *Introduction to Religious Education.* New York: Macmillan, 1932.
Raffety, W. E. *The Smaller Sunday School Makes Good.* Philadelphia: American Sunday School Union, 1927.
Roberts, S. L. *Teaching in the Church School.* Philadelphia: Judson, 1930.Schmauk, T. E. *How to Teach in Sunday School.* Philadelphia: United Lutheran Publication House, 1920.
Smith, R. S. *New Trails for the Christian Teacher.* Philadelphia: Westminster, 1934.
Vieth, P. H. *How to Teach in the Church School.* Philadelphia: Westminster, 1935.
———. *Teaching for Christian Living.* St. Louis: Bethany, 1929.

2

Frank E. Gaebelein
Christian Education in a Democracy
(1951)

The life of a man reflects his inner beliefs—not those to which he gives outward reverence but those which actually dominate his actions.

Evangelical Christian Education

About Frank E. Gaebelein

Frank Ely Gaebelein (1899–1983) was born in Mount Vernon, New York. He was raised in a Christian household, and later in life he was ordained a deacon and presbyter in the Reformed Episcopal Church. Although he never received formal religious training, through his independent study, research, and writing he is considered by some as the most influential evangelical Christian educator of the mid-twentieth century.[1]

Due to his exposure to music, fine arts, and culture, Gaebelein developed a profound interest in the arts and the subject of aesthetics—personally, scholastically, and professionally. His influence in this area can still be seen in the current curriculum of The Stony Brook School, a college-preparatory school he founded in Stony Brook, Long Island, New York. He served as headmaster for forty-one years (1922–1963).

Gaebelein believed in the integration of faith, living, and learning. Cheryl Fawcett and Jamie Thompson write that "Gaebelein was widely known as a Christian humanist because of his insistence that a full education include the arts as well as the sciences and humanities."[2]

Gaebelein believed that the Bible was the perfect foundation of a liberal arts or humanities education.[3]

But he also withstood the pressures of his more fundamentalist brethren. Gaebelein represented the *new evangelical*, who demonstrated "an adherence to orthodoxy and an interest in the sociological problems of the day."[4]

He once stated, "My father was a strong believer in grace, not law. So my home was less legalistic than some other fundamentalist ones."[5]

---

1. Burges, *Models*, 364.
2. Fawcett and Thompson, "Frank E. Gaebelein. See also Gaebelein and Lockerbie, eds., *The Christian, the Arts, and Truth*.
3. "The Creator, The Creation."
4. Fawcett and Thompson, "Frank E. Gaebelein."
5. Ibid. See also Rausch *Arno C. Gaebelein*, 259.

Frank E. Gaebelein

In keeping with Gaebelein's more moderate and social concern tendencies, at the age of seventy he joined the 1965 civil rights march in Selma, Alabama, led by Rev. Martin Luther King Jr.[6]

In addition to his writings and tenure at The Stony Brook School, he also served as an editor for *The New Scofield Reference Bible*, *Christianity Today*, and *The Expositor's Bible Commentary*.

About Christian Education in a Democracy

Gaebelein served as chair of the Commission on Educational Institutions for the National Association of Evangelicals. He developed a comprehensive statement on the philosophy of Christian education. This statement was published as *Christian Education in a Democracy*.[7]

Primarily a manifesto, *Christian Education in Democracy* challenges progressive education by presenting a Christian education world/life-view. He presents his perspective of developing a Christian approach to education blending together liberal and fine arts. While he did all the writing, "The committee argued for the revival of a distinctly Christian approach to learning and teaching with a high priority on the liberal and fine arts."[8]

---

6. Fawcett and Thompson, "Frank E. Gaebelein." See also Gaebelein, "Evangelicals and Social Action."

7. Anthony and Benson, *Exploring the History & Philosophy of Christian Education*, 364.

8. Fawcett and Thompson, "Frank E. Gaebelein." See also Gaebelein and Lockerbie, *The Christian, the Arts, and Truth*.

Evangelical Christian Education

Selected Text:
"Preface to Christian Education"[9]

1

Shortly after the turn of the century, the late Dr. David Starr Jordan, then President of Leland Stanford University, published a lecture, entitled "The Call of the Twentieth Century."[10]

In its pages he ventured upon prophecy; the new century, he said, was not only the threshold of great scientific advances, it would also witness the realization of long-awaited reforms and the establishment of the era of universal peace and prosperity. What Dr. Jordan stated thus early was developed and expanded by many other influential thinkers. Despite the setback of the First World War, the ideas of progress and human perfectibility were dominant in the twenties and thirties. Naturalism, or at most a mild theism based on evolutionary presuppositions, held sway over a majority of educated minds.

But we are living in mid-twentieth-century days. The easy assumptions of the older optimism have been toppled, regardless of their religious convictions or lack of convictions, have been faced with the dark reality of a world rushing toward tragedy so great as to stagger the imagination. The suspicion is abroad with growing force that these are apocalyptic days for Western Civilization and perhaps the whole world. Titles of books and articles tell the story. To name a few, Norman Cousins writes on *Modern Man Is Obsolete*, Howard Mumford Jones on *Education and World Tragedy*, and Harrison Brown asks *Must Destruction Be Our Destiny?* Modern writing is increasingly preoccupied with frustration, disorientation, and despair. The contemporary psychoneurotic school of fiction is a give-away of the increasing insecurity of the modern mind, while in popular reading the juxtaposition of books of religion with the lush historical novel and the hard-boiled detective story is a symptom of the same fumbling grasp for reality.

And so, if this is, as some one has characterized it, 'a lost, suffering, sinful world,' we must in all honesty add a fourth

---

9. In Gaebelein, *Christian Education in a Democracy*.
10. Published by the American Unitarian Association, Boston, 1903.

adjective—fear-ridden. Writing in *Common Sense*, the French author Albert Camus calls this century the century of fear.[11] The same thought is expressed very personally by E. B. White, who begins a letter to the editor of *The New York Herald Tribune* with this sentence: 'I am a member of a party of one, and I live in an age of fear.'[12]

But what neither Mr. Camus nor Mr. White, nor, for that matter, many another modern, cares to acknowledge is the reason for the fear that has seized upon man. Yet the cause is not far to seek. Having long since given up the fear of the Lord, our Western civilization, bowing at the altar of materialism, has substituted for the fear of God the fear of man. Today that terse warning, so often overlooked, of Jesus to His disciples, 'Beware of men,'[13] takes on a new and terrible meaning.

2

Physiography speaks of certain types of terrain as drowned valleys. Today we see the spectacle of a drowned civilization, a culture which, originally owing much to Christianity, has now been thoroughly inundated by the deluge of secularism. Western civilization seems in the process of almost complete de-Christianization. And, while this is going on, man thinks to meet the greatest problems in history with no other resource than himself. The naïve comment of a popular columnist after the explosion of the first atomic bomb, to the effect that we must all, now that the atomic age is here, have more faith in man, is echoed in the closing words of a letter put out by the Emergency Committee of Atomic Scientists of which Albert Einstein was Chairman: 'Sustained by faith in man's ability to control his destiny through the exercise of reason, we have pledged all our strength and knowledge to this work.'[14]

Turning particularly to our own country, we face a paradox. With the future of Western civilization in the balances, millions of us

---

11. Quoted by J. Donald Adams in *The New York Times Book Review*, December 21, 1947.

12. *New York Herald Tribune*, December 2, 1947.

13. Matthew 10:17.

14. Quoted in *The Presbyterian*, March 22, 1947, p. 3.

Evangelical Christian Education

still hold as a working religion little more than what Professor Chad Walsh of Beloit College calls 'secular optimism.' Being rich and increased with goods, we retain an underlying trust in Mammon. The man on the street, though frightened, hopes that through industrial potential and through atomic armament, plus faith in democracy and lip service to God, we shall somehow get by and weather the storm.

But America has not always been secular. To visualize a few sources of our spiritual heritage—the Puritan settlers of New England and the Methodist circuit riders—is to bring to mind how far we have traveled. The path we have taken may be symbolized in the history of our colleges. Harvard, while avoiding sectarianism from the beginning, was called into being, according to its charter of 1650, to educate 'the English and Indian youth of this country in knowledge and godliness,' an aim summed up in its twin mottos of *Veritas* and *Christo et Ecclesiae*. At its founding in 1701, Yale declared its aim to be the preparation of young men for public employment in Church and civil state. Dartmouth was begun to give Christian training to 'savages.' That at these institutions initial religious purpose has long since given way to secularism is no more debatable than the fact that almost every other American college of similar foundation has followed the same road.

Nor are the colleges alone in their secularization. Once the home with grace at meals, family prayers, and loyalty to the church, could to a significant degree be counted upon to provide children with a spiritual heritage. But now the typical American home is a secular institution, and the typical child receives little, if any, positive religious teaching. In a notable article published in *The Atlantic Monthly* in 1924,[15] President Eliot of Harvard pointed out that there were in America at that time 'tens of millions of men and women of scanty education who are not connected with any church and, apparently, take no interest in any religious doctrine of practice. Their children are not baptized or christened. . . . Children get no religious instruction whatever at home or abroad and grow to maturity without knowledge of Christianity or any other religion and densely ignorant of the fundamental moralities and good manners. No such experiment on so vast a scale has ever been tried since time began as this

---

15. Cf. *The Atlantic Monthly*, March 1924. Used by permission.

considerable fraction of the American people is not trying—namely, bringing up their children without any religious instruction . . .' But, were President Eliot writing now, he would have to leave out the qualifying phrase, 'of scanty education,' because college graduates are today in the forefront of present-day secularism. As for the multitude of unchurched young people in the United States, it has increased until it now stands at no less than 27,000,000 of our youth. Dorothea Brand in characterizing them cuts deep when she writes: 'The moving picture house is the church of the modern adolescent; the novel his Bible; and he turns to the tabloid newspaper for the lesson of the day.'[16] In 1949 there were 1,763,290 serious crimes committed in the United States, and the predominant age in the frequency of arrests was twenty-one. Yet could anything else be expected with the ratio of divorces to marriages about one to three and the nation spending eight times as much on alcoholic beverages as on all churches and benevolences put together?

We are, however, concerned with education. And so the question arises: What of education in relation to the dilemma of America and of the world? The fact is that, as both home and church have lost their grip on American youth, the people of this country have looked to education to fill the gap. With a confidence that would be touching were it not based on evasion of responsibility, they have turned their youth—body, mind, and soul—over to the most extensive and highly organized system of education that the world has ever known. The result has hardly been a happy one. The plain record, not only of juvenile but also of adult delinquency, cries aloud the failure of secularized education to do its part in developing character and personality adequate to stand the tensions of life today. As Dr. Allan V. Heely, Headmaster of the Lawrenceville School, has put it: 'The problem of American education is not to secure adequate financing, it is to set up a system of schools good enough to be worth financing.'[17] And here is the principal of a great suburban high school, Dr. Howard G. Spalding of Mount Vernon, N.Y., writing a leading article in *School and Society* on 'Education and the Crisis in Character.' After a forthright reference to the slump in national morality as shown by the

---

16. Quoted in Watts, *The Incomparable Book*, 220.
17. *New York Times*, February 16, 1945.

Evangelical Christian Education

breakdown in marriage, towering liquor bills, dishonest citizenship manifest in black markets, and the callousness of both workers and employees to the rights of their fellow citizens, he says: 'We who teach must view these evidences of lack of character with special concern. These adults who wreck their home, seek wealth by dishonest means, and violate all of the laws of God and man are our former pupils. In part we made them what they are. We believe in the power of education, yet clearly that power has not been great enough to build a morally sound nation.'[18]

But why have our schools failed in the development of moral character? They have failed because there has been ruled out of them the only dynamic able to produce character tough enough to weather an ethical climate where the winds blow in the direction of moral short cuts and easy self-indulgence. From trying to make God an elective subject, public education has now been brought to the pass of refusing to give God even so much as elective status. All this has been done in the name of the essential principle of separation of Church and State and in behalf of freedom from authoritarianism. The result is that the Bible, the greatest moral and spiritual source book in the world, has no place on the required reading list of our American youth.

Yet may we honestly fall back upon the principle of separation of Church and State as justification of this great divorce of God from American education? Against the background of the Supreme Court decision in the Champaign-McCollum case, these words of Dean Emeritus Luther B. Weigle of Yale Divinity School are prophetic: 'The principle of religious freedom which insures the separation of church and state is precious. It touches bedrock in its truth. It is a guarantee of our liberties. But the principle of the separation of church and state must not be construed so as to render the state a fosterer of non- religion or atheism. Yet that is precisely what we are doing in America today.'[19] It obviously is not the purpose of this book to plead for the intrusion of denominational religion into public education, a process inconsistent with the American spirit. But we cannot avoid

---

18. *School and Society*, March 29, 1947.
19. Quoted in Howlett, ed., *Religion, the Dynamic of Education*, 18.

protesting the progressive surrender of the public school to the forces of irreligion, with results that are all too apparent.

What then of independent education? Surely the commitment of the public school to a program of education without God presents a challenge to the spiritual freedom of independent or private schools. It reminds us that, bound by few of the limitations that restrict public education, independent schools and colleges enjoy full liberty to teach religion in general and Christianity in particular—or for that matter, any other faith. Today parents who would have their children under religious tutelage must turn back to the Church and the home, the two institutions which, by their progressive abdication of responsibility for spiritual training, have done much to bring about the present situation. And if they desire to supplement the teaching of home and Church, an increasing number will be looking to nonpublic institutions.

Certainly the day of uncritical faith in the power of secular education to develop youth capable of meeting the overwhelming stress of our times is gone. These fifties in which we are living prove the inadequacy of the truncated education which refuses to deal with the soul as well as with the mind of man. One of the leading systems of education in Europe was that of pre-Nazi Germany. Yet Emil Brunner placed his finger on its Achilles' heel when he replied to the question why a nation such as Germany with its long Christian tradition and with its contribution of spiritual leadership in the past should turn to outright paganism: 'Ah, there is where you make your mistake. The paganism of Germany was not a sudden thing. For over half a century God and religion have been gradually disappearing from the schools of Germany. Education has become secular. A generation has arisen which acknowledges no God and no longer regards those basic moral sanctions which are the safeguard of national and international harmony and decency. That is why the churches of Germany are empty and the nation has turned its face toward the darkness in the wake of Adolph Hitler.'[20] And as for the Orient, Japan was by all odds the most advanced nation educationally in the Far East, yet she was not thereby saved from ruin. Mere literacy, no matter how high

20. From an address before the Presbyterian (U.S.) Synod of Virginia, 1941.

its rate throughout a nation, is only a tool capable of good or bad uses as it expresses the will of a people.

3

What then is the answer to the dilemma of education today? For dilemma there certainly is. The fact that colleges and universities all over the country have been working out and, in some instances, have published various philosophies of education and curriculum revisions reveals not only an attitude of wholesome self-criticism but also a significant uncertainty regarding the integrating factor of education. The National Citizens Commission for the Public Schools is engaged in a six-year inquiry into our educational system. Articles, some critical and others laudatory, on the public schools, are appearing in national magazines. The problems of education are of widespread concern. And the search goes on for a single over-all concept that will bring unity amid the conflicting aims and objectives of modern education.

But is an answer possible? To put it very definitely, can anyone or any group of persons have the temerity to claim to have found the unifying factor which will bring ultimate meaning and drive to education and which will give promise of producing in American youth that character without which the survival of democracy is imperiled? To reply in the affirmative to a question like that demands humility. Any group of scholars, no matter how highly accomplished, would hesitate a long time before making such a claim for its own original findings. But if it can sincerely and with compelling logic recall education to the path from which it wandered long ago, provided that the path was the right one, then the claim takes on another hue. Let us grant that the path is an old one, that it is based upon certain great truths found in full power only in the Bible, and that the modern mind shies away from the Scriptural and theological. The fact remains that the only criterion for the path education must take is neither popularity nor 'modernity,' but eternal truth.

At this point someone may object: 'You are advocating a return to a unifying factor which may have been valid a hundred years ago. But that is impossible. Life has changed. The old beliefs no longer hold water. Modern industrial, scientific civilization has outmoded the religious concepts upon which our earlier education was based. We could not return to that unifying factor if we would.' Or, as the Harvard Report says with urbane finality: 'But whatever one's views, religion is not now for most colleges or universities a practical source of intellectual unity.'[21]

The idea, however, is not so easily interred. For its facile dismissal rests upon the misconception, so dear to modern intellectual pride, that Christianity as a unifying factor of education is dead because man today has passed beyond it. In short, it is believed that the widened horizons of modern science have made a genuinely Christian world-view irrelevant. That is a very great error. It amounts to nothing less than saying that Christ and the Bible have no relevancy for our times. Nothing could be more blind and false. For nearly two thousand years He has been the Contemporary of all that is enduring and spiritual in man.

To those in every age who are committed above all else to doing the will of God He has ever been closer 'than breathing and nearer than hands and feet.' And the Book which is the great source of knowledge of Him and of His way of Life is one which, under the most withering persecutions any book has ever endured, has obstinately refused to die.

One thing is sure. Education as well as civilization has lost the way. The sentence with which Dante began *The Divine Comedy* applies to us: 'In the middle of the journey of this life, I came to myself in a dark wood, where the direct way was lost.' Whether we like it or not, we are now in that dark wood. Our generation has lost the direct way. But the way is there, even the Way which before the disciples were ever called Christians, was the earliest designation of the faith of Him who declared Himself the Way, the Truth, and the Life. To get back on it will require arduous cutting through of accretions of secular prejudice and the resolute following of directions none too congenial to an age in which material progress is preferred to spiritual values; above all, it will require repentance even to the humbling of our humanistic pride and the acknowledgment that, despite our great scientific achievements, we are wandering in the night. But it is

---

21. *General Education in a Free Society*, 39.

the only way; and, if education is to have any hope of leading youth safely through the dark wood of our age, it must lose no time in coming to itself.

4

So much for the climate of opinion and the dilemma of education today. Let us now come directly to the subject of this book. Its title, *Christian Education in a Democracy* imposes certain obligations. Exactly what is meant by 'Christian education' on the one hand and 'democracy' on the other hand? Clearly something in the way of definition is needed. If the chapters that follow are to be read with understanding, the two poles of thought round which they are organized must be seen not only individually but also in their dependence one upon the other. Thus a word about relationship is in order.

This book deals with a particular kind of education, which we call 'Christian,' moreover it deals with it in a certain setting, namely, 'democracy.' In the nature of the case, the latter will be less to the fore than the former; the setting, while essential, remains background, not subject. But though the background is subordinate, it may well be given prior consideration. The relation of the two, subject and background, is by no means simple. Such painting as that in which the old Dutch masters excelled comes to mind—an exquisitely drawn goblet of rare glass, some richly colored fruit, set against a spotless tablecloth. Artists call this 'still life,' the objects depicted being lifeless and inert. And being inert, the subject and background can have no mutual interaction. Better by way of analogy would be the portrait of a living man with his study or office as setting. Still better would be a father and mother painted with their children in the background. For here a living reciprocity between subject and setting is portrayed. So with the subject of this book and its social context; the relationship is likewise organic. Christian education exists, not as a theological or philosophical speculation, but in a society of living, breathing human beings. This society, as it is known to us in America, is free and democratic; and between it and Christian education, there is constantly going on a living interchange, spiritually, intellectually, and physically.

Frank E. Gaebelein

We turn, then, to democracy as the setting for Christian education. As we begin to think about the meaning of the term, the qualifying word 'American' comes to mind. Though unexpressed in the title, it is American democracy with which this volume is to deal. Therefore we ask the question: What is the democracy? What kind of democratic society is it which is peculiar to the United States? To speak glibly of the American way of life, or of our 'free society,' is only to substitute catch-phrases for comprehension of the roots, origin, and present state of the social and political environment in which we are living.

We need to remind ourselves that American democracy was not a sudden development; it was not Minerva, springing full grown from the head of Zeus, let along from the heads of Washington, Jefferson, and the other founding fathers. On the contrary, it has an ancestry whose most important member provides a link between democracy today and the kind of education with which this book is concerned. For it is neither religious dogmatism nor sectarian bias but simple fidelity to truth to state that a major source, if not the taproot itself, of democracy is the Protestant tradition, grounded in the Christianity of the Bible.

Consider the relationship of the Reformation to the beginnings of America. Though one of the undeniable facts of history, this relationship is little appreciated today, thanks to the caricature of Reformed doctrine by teachers and writers ignorant of its grandeur. With his rediscovery of evangelical truth and his insistence upon individual responsibility, Martin Luther laid many of the foundations upon which our political freedom rests. And John Calvin went on to build a system of theology and church polity which decisively affected the development of our democracy. The famous sentence of Leopold von Ranke, 'John Calvin was the virtual founder of America,' has been echoed in various ways by other historians, including Bancroft, D'Aubigne, Taine, Buckle, Motley, and Fiske.

It was no accident that the Mecklenburg Declaration of 1775, some of the words of which were used by Thomas Jefferson in 1776, was drafted by a score of Scotch-Irish Calvinists in North Carolina. Of course, Jefferson was himself a deist, and the influence of the French Enlightenment entered strongly into the political philosophy that shaped the Declaration of Independence and the Constitution.

Evangelical Christian Education

Nevertheless, religiously speaking, a leading influence upon our Revolution was the evangelical one of Calvinism. As Horace Walpole ruefully put it, 'Cousin America has run off with a Presbyterian parson.'[22]

There were other evangelical influences, as in Rhode Island, where Baptist influence was dominant and where democracy was early practiced. Nor is this all. A major factor in the subsequent development of our freedom was John Wesley. That the revival he began saved England from a revolution like that in France is a truism. He did more; he awakened the conscience of his country. The mighty movement that he headed renewed the moral and spiritual life of England and America and channeled the power of evangelicalism into social action.

But let us return to the present. As for American society today, it is no utopia. Theoretically, the democracy based on the Constitution and the Bill of Rights is a towering monument of political wisdom. Actually, our democracy is on another level. The faults of America spring from the incomplete application of sound political doctrine and the imperfect embodiment of Christian principles. But however great these faults may be, in a world still in good part politically enslaved ours is a free society, the members of which enjoy such basic rights as freedom of religion, speech, and assembly. Like all human institutions, democracy is not static. It is responsive to human needs, growing, changing, making mistakes, yet continuing free. Short of theocracy it offers the greatest possibilities for the development of human personality.

In the forefront of the liberties guaranteed American citizens is that of religion. Along with freedom of worship Christian education exists in our society by constitutional right. And the support of our democracy is not only a patriotic duty but also a Christian obligation. The New Testament is very clear in regard to what a Christian man owes the state.[23] Yet when all is said and done, American democracy, however much we love and honor it, remains a fallible, human institution, rendering at the most a formal obeisance to the Deity.

---

22. Cf. for the background of these two paragraphs, Boettner, *The Reformed Doctrine of Predestination*, ch. 28, pp. 7–8.

23. Matthew 22:21; Romans 13:1–7.

Frank E. Gaebelein

The distinction just made between democratic principle and practice leads to the realization that society in America is not Christian. The life of a man reflects his inner beliefs—not those to which he gives outward reverence but those which actually dominate his actions. By this token the majority of Americans are not Christian believers in any vital sense of the term. As Professor Commager shows in *The American Mind*, the average citizen of this republic is a thoroughly secular person—materialistic and definitely of this world.

That the relation between Christian education and a society of this kind includes certain tensions is inevitable. From the beginning Christianity has not been at home in its worldly environment. Although it goes on in a worldly setting, Christian education also stands apart from the world, which in America means from this secularized society. Not that physical isolation is implied. The separation is spiritual, not material; the nonconformity is within and finds expression in purity of life rather than in withdrawal from human contacts. Asceticism is neither in the mainstream of Protestantism nor of apostolic Christianity. The true function in the world of the individual Christian as well as of the Church is summed up in the declaration, 'Ye are the salt of the earth.'[24] Salt can be a preservative only as it affects its environment. So also with Christian education; it too must interact with this American democracy in the midst of which it is called upon to do its work.

5

We are now ready to shift our attention from background to subject. And it will help the transition to look once more at the title, *Christian Education in a Democracy*. Several questions come to mind. What field of education is in view? What is meant by 'Christian' education? Though here the adjective is obviously of key importance, something should also be said of the noun. Its meaning, though so definitely modified by 'Christian,' is not thereby confined to specialized branches of Christian training like the theological seminary, the Bible school, or the Sunday school. It comprehends the whole field from elementary to higher education. Nor is it limited to private or

---

24. Matthew 5:13.

public institutions, but rather it concerns both. Moreover, certain out-of-school but immensely important aspects of education, such as the home and various forms of adult education, are within its scope.

But to return to the adjective. In what sense should the term Christian education be understood? Is it generally the same as 'religious' education? Or does it carry some special denominational shade of meaning? In reply, let it be said at once that the word 'Christian' is something more than a pious synonym for 'religious.' There are many religions; there is only one Christianity. The faith of the apostles and their successors through the ages is not just one among a number of world religions; instead, it is nothing less than the revelation of God to a lost world. Though there is truth in the ethnic religions, between them and Christianity there stands the immeasurable gulf of difference in kind as well as degree.

Compare, for example, the Founder of Christianity with the other great religious leaders. Whether it be Buddha, Confucius, Mohammed, or even Moses, when these great men are put beside Christ, He is seen to be of a wholly different order of life. A Christian is first of all an individual to whom Jesus is God. For the believer his Lord is not in competition with any other spiritual leader; he knows that Jesus is the God-man, the unique Son of the Father, the Saviour of the world. From the very first century, this has been the unbroken testimony of all true Christians. As Robert E. Speer put it in the closing words of his greatest book: 'On this Rock of Jesus Christ, the Son of God and the Son of Man, the only Redeemer, Saviour and Lord, the Christian church stood at the beginning. Here it has stood through all the ages. Here it must continue to stand.... From this foundation the Church of Christ, so long as it is true to its message and its mission, whether at home or abroad, will never remove.'[25]

In a day when thinking about theology tends to be foggy, distinctions such as these need emphasis. Much that passes for Christian education in American schools and colleges is nothing more than well-intentioned morality and kindly altruism. That these are valid religious outcomes no one doubts. But neither morality nor altruism is peculiar to Christianity, and the education that does not go beyond ethics is sub-Christian, whatever its label. By any incisive

25. Speer, *The Finality of Jesus Christ*, 377.

Frank E. Gaebelein

definition, a great deal of what, even in church-related institutions, passes for Christian education never rises above the level of benevolent moralism.

And yet, along with insistence upon the unique content of the word 'Christian,' there goes a true inclusiveness. No one denomination has a monopoly upon that noble name 'Christian.' It belongs to every Church that gives preeminence to the Lord Jesus Christ and that derives from the inspired Word its worship and service of God. At this point it becomes necessary to combine breadth of outlook with precision of thought. The sponsorship of this volume, while not denominational, may be descried by the venerable term 'evangelical.' The word comes into English straight from the passages of the Greek New Testament, where '*euangelion*' is the common word for 'gospel.' According to authoritative definition, 'evangelical' describes 'what the majority of Protestants regard as the fundamental doctrines of the gospel, such as personal union with Christ, the Trinity, the fallen condition of man, Christ's atonement fro sin, salvation by faith, not by works, and regeneration y the Holy Spirit.[26] It is not a denominational term. By this definition, St. Paul and other apostles were evangelicals, as were St. Augustine, Luther, and Calvin. So were Latimer and Bunyan, Roger Williams and Jonathan Edwards, Wesley and Whitfield, Philips Brooks and Liddon, Spurgeon and Moody. The evangelical faith comprises those great doctrines common to all orthodox sections of Protestantism, doctrines that it finds in the Bible, received as the Book given throughout by inspiration of God.

Such are the principles of evangelical Christianity. And, it may be added, the experience of the committee responsible for this volume bears witness to the breadth of fellowship possible on this basis. Its members, though drawn from many denominations, have submerged individual differences, so that Armenians and Calvinists, Baptists and paedo-Baptists, adherents of various kinds of church government, have co-operated on the common ground of inspired Scripture, the great truths of redemption, and Christian life and service.

But while evangelicalism breaks through denominational lines, it is at the same time distinct from other views that, in parallel fashion,

26. Funk & Wagnalls *Practical Standard Dictionary* (New York, 1924).

Evangelical Christian Education

also go beyond these lines. For there is a world of difference between evangelical Christianity and such views as neo-orthodoxy and modernism. The former, despite its emphasis on man's sin and his need of redemption, denies the full inspiration of the Bible; the latter, with its tendency toward a naturalistic interpretation of Christianity and its repudiation of inspiration, is less concerned with sin and the need of personal redemption than with the innate perfectibility of man and the building of a new order by human efforts.

Of course, 'liberalism,' in the non-theological sense of the fight for human freedom and social betterment, is by no means the exclusive possession of those who repudiate the historic Christianity of the Bible. Despite the lag of some of its present-day followers in concern for the needs of society, the faith that nurtured foreign-missions movement, fathered our greatest universities, cared for the outcasts in city slums, and out of which revivals have been born, need no apology.

It is with this evangelical faith, not simply as another system of theology but as the unifying factor of Christian education, that this book is concerned. In a sense, it is a summons to return to a position that is old and at the same time new. There are times when the only way forward is to go back. Not every truth, past or present, is that set forth in the New Testament. Whatever men have done is overlaying its plain meaning with tradition, the Gospel of Jesus Christ is still the most revolutionary force in the life of mankind. Of all the figures of antiquity, Christ is the only one who is living today and is beckoning us on toward a new and brighter world.

No sensible person would want education to beat a retreat to the colleges of colonial days or even of the nineteenth century, Christian as most of them were. 'The letter killeth, but the Spirit giveth life.'[27] The particular studies and educational methods of a former age may have little meaning for today, but the Gospel which Robert Bridges at the close of *The Testament of Beauty* called the

> only deathless athanasian creed,—the which 'except a man believe he cannot be saved'

---

27. 2 Corinthians 3:6.

remains the greatest liberating power in the world. 'Ye shall know the truth, and the truth shall make you free'[28] is the master text of Christian education. And, though modern science and philosophy have taken it over, neither has any exclusive right to it. For almost in the next breath Jesus went on to say: 'If the Son therefore shall make you free, you shall be free indeed.'[29] It is spiritual truth, embodied in the Son of God, that strikes the shackles from men. It is Christ alone who quickens men's hearts and emancipates them from evil. There is more to the good life than the intellect. St. Paul was voicing universal experience when he cried out: The good that I would, I do not: but the evil which I would not, that I do[30]—which is akin to the conflict Ovid had in mind when he said: 'I see the better, and approve and—choose the worse.'[31] The same problem is with us now, terribly aggravated through the stupendous destructive powers of modern man. And still, as in the first century, it demands for its resolution One who is stronger than evil, more powerful than sin, great enough to change the human heart. St. Bernard knew who that was, when he declared: 'My highest philosophy is to know Jesus and Jesus crucified.' So speaks every Christian. There is nothing narrow about this answer to the search for the unifying principle of education. Jesus Christ is not a sectarian Person; bigger than any human attempt to define His significance, He is Himself the answer. Education is not theory, it is life; and the truest solution of its problem lies not in abstract principles but in a living Person.

And so, while our call to education is a call back to the Bible and Christ, it is at the same time a summons to go forward with Him. In Him is the life more abundant, the highest goal of education. His greatest victories are yet to come. He is Lord of the future as well as of the past. For He alone can declare, 'I am he that liveth and was dead; and behold, I am alive forevermore.'[32]

28. John 8:32.
29. John 8:36.
30. Romans 7:19.
31. *Metamorphoses*, book 7, lines 20–21.
32. Revelation 1:18.

6

Something should now be said regarding those for whom this book is meant. It is not 'Christian Education for a Democracy,' but 'Christian Education in a Democracy' which is in view. The former would imply the setting up of Christian education as a requirement for all American youth. However much we believe in evangelical, Protestant education, it would be highly unrealistic to expect that such education be given to all, or to the majority, or even to a very large minority of our youth. While for believers Christianity is the final faith, in a democracy it is one of a number of religions. While for evangelicals, historic, Bible-centered Protestantism is the purest form of Christianity, in a democracy it does not enjoy a jot more privilege than Roman or Greek Catholicism, Mormonism, or Christian Science.

Granted all this, there yet remains a significant area of education in America to be challenged. By no means all the schools in America are public. Many are private or independent. As for the colleges, still more are independent. And it is this influential and growing section of American education which should find the chapters that follow of direct concern.

Beyond the circle of readers engaged professionally in formal education, there is the vast sector of Protestantism committed to the evangelical faith and including believers among the Methodists, Baptists, Lutherans, Congregationalist, Episcopalians, Presbyterian and Reformed Churches, and many other groups. To many of these this presentation of Christian education will be of personal interest because of their participation in such activities as the Sunday school or various forms of adult Christian work. The welfare of their children gives others a personal stake in the problems of education. And last of all this book is designed to compel the respectful consideration of some who, in accord with the secular spirit of the times, have nothing more than a historical interest in Christianity, if that. It is hoped that their open-minded reading of these pages will show them that for modern education Christianity is a living issue.

This, then, is a manifesto, not a mere dispassionate survey. On controversial questions it takes sides. Like all Christian witness, it seeks a verdict. Its sponsors are quite aware that its appeal is not a majority one. But they have faith in the power of a dedicated minority. They know that Christian history abounds with examples of the decisive influence of the devoted few: an 'Athanasius contra mundum,' a Luther at Worms, a Carey attempting and accomplishing great things for God, a Niemoeller defying a Hitler—these are only some of a noble army. Men and women, administrators and teachers, schools and colleges willing to go all the way in Christian education may not be numerous; but under God their influence may yet tip the balances in favor of the spiritual revitalization needed to bring America victoriously through the ordeal of this age.

3

Findley B. Edge
Teaching for Results (1956)

The teacher needs some plan to find out whether the lives of the members are really being influenced by his teaching. Admittedly, this is difficult to do. But in too many instances teachers have no idea whether or not their teaching is making any significant difference in the lives of their class members.

Findley B. Edge

About Findley B. Edge

Little is written about Findley Edge, the man, yet his impact on evangelical Christian education is significant. Findley Bartow Edge (1916–2002) was born in Albany, Georgia. He remained a lifelong Southern Baptist. Edge maintained a relationship with Southern Baptist Theological Seminary for over forty years, including as professor from 1947 to 1984.[1]

About Teaching for Results

Teaching For Results was a standard text in seminaries for more than forty years. First printed in 1956, it is still in print today. It is both a comprehensive and practical resource for evangelical Christian educators. According to Yates and Purcell, before terms like "purpose-driven" or "high expectations" were standard clichés, "Findley Edge's book, *Teaching for Results*, brought to the forefront a critical question in the field of teaching: 'What is your goal?' . . . It is unequaled in its simplicity in teaching the Sunday school teacher how to establish and achieve goals. . . . Findley Edge was a pioneer in this area long before they were common phrases."[2]

As one reads this book, it becomes apparent rather quickly that many contemporary popular Christian education books, perhaps unbeknownst to the respective authors, have their roots in *Teaching for Results*.

Selected Text: "Securing Carry-Over"[3]

We have said that one of the problems we confront in teaching in the Sunday school is that the lesson does not sufficiently carry over into the lives of the class members. Probably one reason for this is that the teacher does not make specific plans for a carry-over to take place. In concluding the lesson, the teacher often makes some

1. Yates and Purcell, "Findley B. Edge."
2. Ibid.
3. Ch. 5 in Edge, *Teaching for Results*.

general application of it and exhorts the class to comply. Or, in some instances, the bell rings before the lesson is finished, and the teacher is forced to make some hurried, concluding comments before the class is dismissed. If the teacher expects to secure definite results from his teaching, something more than this is needed.

Plan for Carry-Over

Teachers often fail to secure results because no plans were made for results to be obtained. Too often, the teacher leaves the results "up in the air." The time to remedy this is when the lesson is being prepared. Securing carry-over should be as definite a part of the lesson plan as the development of the lesson or making the lesson personal.

Carry-over involves two things: first, a decision by the class concerning what can and should be done; second, a plan for definite action. It may be either individual or group action, depending on the nature of the project. A class of Juniors may decide to start reading their Bibles daily; this would involve individual action. A class of young adults may decide to sponsor a recreation program for the young people in the church; this would involve group action. The response will take place outside the classroom, but the decision for action and at least the initial plan for action must take place within the classroom.

In the teacher's lesson plan, there should be a section headed "How to Secure Carry-Over." When the teacher determines what specific conduct response he would like the class members to make as the result of the teaching of this lesson, he also plans how he will lead the group to choose this response as their own.

The response decided upon by the class should be acted upon immediately. Of course, there will be times when it is impossible for the group to react to a spiritual truth that quickly. Months or even years may pass before the full fruit of the teaching may be seen. But teachers have leaned too heavily upon this concept and too often have used it as an excuse for poor and ineffective teaching. The teacher should try to make his teaching and the response so specific that the class members will be able to begin demonstrating an evidence of the spiritual truth in their lives during the following week.

Findley B. Edge

Members Make Their Own Suggestions

While the teacher must make definite plans for this carry-over, it is far better for the class members to make their own suggestions as to what they can and will do the following week. How may a teacher accomplish this result? It must be remembered that action imposed by an outside authority (such as the teacher) probably will not be meaningful in the experience of the group. For the decision or course of action to be meaningful to the individual, the individual must choose it for himself. This is eminently true in the realm of moral attitudes or spiritual action.

Three things should be kept in mind: In the first place, while the teacher may make plans for a certain response by class members, it is entirely possible for the members of the class to choose a different response. If the response chosen by the class is worthy and Christian, it is entirely acceptable. In fact, it will be better than the one the teacher had in mind because it is their idea. Of course, the teacher might have several possible responses in mind, and each individual in the class could come to a different response in light of his own particular need and interest. Such decisions would be both legitimate and worthy, for the teacher would not have imposed his idea upon the class, and their responses would be individually chosen.

In the second place, even though the teacher makes the suggestion as to a possible response, it is possible for the class to select this response for themselves. A father may come home on a hot summer afternoon and say to his two boys, "Let's go swimming." If the boys reply enthusiastically, "Oh, boy! Let's do!" The has not imposed his will on the boys. Their response is just as surely self-chosen as if the boys had made the suggestion themselves.

In the third place, it is important that the response have meaning for the learner. For that to occur, the learner must have insight into both the situation he confronts and the desired response in that situation. He must clearly see the issues involved in a given response. He must be made aware of the conflicting interests, desires, and passions within his own life. Jesus constantly sought to lead his followers to understand what following him involved. "If any man would come after me," he said, adding in effect, let him count the cost.

The learner must not respond on a superficial basis such as to please a teacher. He must be led to face the situation frankly and, in the light of the total commitment of his life to Jesus and of his accepted generalized ideals in this particular situation, to choose what to him seems to be the Christian response. There must be true individual choice with no external pressure exerted. The decision must come from deep within the learner if it is to be either Christian or lasting.

Follow-Up by the Teacher

The teacher needs some plan to find out whether the lives of the members are really being influenced by his teaching. Admittedly, this is difficult to do. But in too many instances teachers have no idea whether or not their teaching is making any significant difference in the lives of their class members. They have only the vague hope that they are "doing some good." If the teacher is to expect results, if he is to obtain results, this vague hope is not sufficient. He must find out what is actually happening in the lives of those whom he teaches. There are several different plans the teacher may use in securing this information. With pre-adolescent children he might simply ask for a report on what they did during the week to carry out the decisions made in class the previous Sunday. If the class decided on a group project, the teacher may observe them at work. With the younger age groups the teacher may have personal conferences with parents or, in parent-teacher meetings, discuss the actions or behavior of the child in the areas in which the teacher has sought conduct response. In certain instances the teacher will be able to sense much of this information through individual, informal talks with the class members.

A plan for follow-up is needed to let the class members know that the teacher really expects them to do something about what is taught on Sunday morning. Some class members have gotten into such a habit of agreeing with what the teacher says without making any definite response to the teaching that they do not realize the teacher really expects them to do something about it. The understanding must be instilled in the minds of the class members that this teaching is for life and for action.

The check-up plan will vary according to the age group. It will be most difficult with a group of adults and easiest with Intermediates, Juniors, and younger children. But regardless of how difficult it may be, if results are to be achieved, a follow-up must be made. This is not to suggest that the teacher be a spy who tries to catch his members when they do not respond properly. It simply means that an interested teacher is vitally concerned whether or not his members are growing as Christians. It means he is not willing to leave his teaching to chance.

An Example

An example might help the reader to understand more clearly how a teacher might go about trying to secure this carry-over. Let us say the teacher is dealing with a class of twelve-year-old boys. He has as his aim, "To lead my class members to be regular in attendance at the morning preaching service for the next quarter." He has led the group in a meaningful study of the Bible and to accept in general the idea that Christian people should worship God regularly. After this, he presents the class with a life situation in which they see something of the difficulty involved in regular church attendance. After further study and discussion, the group accepts the aim that people should worship God regularly in spite of difficulties. The teacher then comes to the carry-over.

> TEACHER: "Do any of you know what percentage of our class attended church regularly last quarter?"
>
> RESPONSE: "No."
>
> TEACHER (writing on the blackboard): "We had only 45 percent."
>
> RESPONSE: "That's not good."
>
> TEACHER: "No, that isn't good. In light of our discussion today what do you think our class percentage for church attendance ought to be next quarter?"
>
> RESPONSE: "It ought to be 100 percent."

TEACHER: "Certainly, that is the ideal. But let us be more realistic. What per cent do you think we actually ought to try to reach for this next quarter?"

RESPONSE: "Eighty-five percent."

RESPONSE: "Sixty percent"

RESPONSE: "Seventy-five percent."

TEACHER: "I see we have different ideas concerning the matter."

After discussion, the class agrees on a certain percentage.

TEACHER: "Now what are we going to do to help ourselves reach this percentage? We haven't reached it in the past, so if we are going to reach it, we will have to do more work than we have been doing. Does anyone have any suggestions that will help us reach this goal?"

RESPONSE: "Let's all sit together at the preaching service this next quarter."

THE REST OF THE CLASS: "Yes. That would be great!"

TEACHER: "All right, I will contact your parents and ask them if that will be agreeable with them. Is there any other suggestion you may have?"

RESPONSE: "We might have a committee to telephone everybody in the class on Saturday and remind them to stay for church on Sunday."

TEACHER: "That is a good suggestion. Who would you like to have on that committee?"

RESPONSE: "I think it is too much to ask one committee to call the members of the class for three whole months. Would it not be better to have three committees and let them phone for only one month each?"

TEACHER: "That is an excellent idea. Then let's select three committees."

Findley B. Edge

The discussion continues until definite and specific plans are made to secure the carry-over in the lives of the class members.

A group of adults might have a lesson on Christian growth. A conduct response aim might be, "To lead each member to engage in a serious, systematic study of the Bible for this quarter." In the traditional approach to this lesson, the teacher would call attention to the fact that one way to grow is through studying the Bible. He would then conclude the lesson with the exhortation, "Let's all study the Bible more." The class would agree but it is likely that the members would make no specific response.

In the approach being suggested here, the teacher would seek to lead the group to make definite plans for carry-over to take place. In developing the lesson and in making the lesson personal, the teacher would lead the group to a commitment to the idea that we need to study the Scriptures more intensively. In the carry-over, the teacher would call attention to the fact that usually a general commitment to Bible study is not sufficient because the press of daily affairs soon crowds it out. He would suggest to the group that they consider setting up a systematic schedule for daily study for one quarter. Various schedules and the problems involved would be considered. What portion of the Bible might be used in this study would also be considered.

The teacher would lead the class to consider what aids they might want to use to make their study of the Bible more understandable and meaningful. Too often the average person becomes discouraged in his study of the Bible because he does not understand what he reads. If the group decides they would like to study the Gospel of John as their project for the next three months, the teacher should have brought from the church library an inexpensive commentary on the New Testament. He should indicate the help it would be to them as an aid in Bible study. Questions would be asked and answered, problems would be raised, and the discussion would continue until specific plans were made for the carry-over to take place.

This is the key to the success of the lesson. This is the point at which the nail is driven up to the head. All of the rest of the lesson has been generalized discussion about what might or should be done. In this portion of the lesson, each member is led to consider *what he is going to do.* Therefore, because this part of the lesson is so important it is necessary for the teacher to save plenty of time. If the bell ends the class session before the conclusion is reached, it is likely the values of the entire lesson will be lost. This conclusion must be unhurried. It takes time for the class members to think, to make decisions, to draw conclusions, and to make specific plans as to what they will do.

It may be that this matter of carry-over is the most important and least used of the entire lesson plan. Many teachers may have a specific objective. They may start with the interest of the group arid lead to a purposeful study of the Bible. They may have an interesting development of the lesson and then make a very practical application of it. But at this point they stop short and fail to secure the carry-over into life experience,

The teacher makes the application and then exhorts the class to practice it in a fashion similar to this: "Christ helped those in need; let us follow his example." Or, "Jesus is our example. Let's try to follow his example." Or, "We are living in a sinful world. Let's try to make our world a better place in which to live." Then the class is dismissed with prayer and no specific plans are made through which the members may carry out the matter discussed in the lesson. As a result, the likelihood is that the members, having agreed with the generalized concept, will go out and do nothing.

In certain instances, the course of action decided on by the class will be too involved for plans to be worked out fully in the class period. In this case, it may be that the class will want to have a special meeting during the week to work out the details of the plan to be followed. Or, the class may appoint a committee to study the problems and report to the class the following Sunday.

A teacher of an adult class had as his aim, "To lead my class to take some positive steps to provide a more wholesome environment for the social life of our high school group." In teaching the lesson he pointed out some of the evils in the community which served as a source of temptation to young people. One of the class members replied that something ought to be done to eliminate these evils and to provide a more positively Christian environment for the high school students. The teacher faced the class with the suggestion, and the class unanimously decided to undertake this as a class project.

Findley B. Edge

This project was, of course, too involved to be worked out in the class period. The class decided to meet at the teacher's home on Tuesday night for discussion and planning. At this meeting, they considered such questions as: What shall be our plan of attack on this problem? What facilities of a Christian nature are available to our young people? What facilities of a questionable nature are available to our young people? What facilities of a distinctly unchristian nature are available to our young people? Shall we make a survey as to where and how our young people spend their leisure time? What committees do we need? Questions were faced. Answers were sought. Other meetings were held. The course of action was decided upon and put into effect.

Planning sessions such as these will not simply end in "talk" or with a general exhortation—"Let's all try to help our young people"—but in action. It could well be that in carrying out a project of this type, the class members might learn more practical Christianity than they would learn from just listening to a teacher for a number of Sundays.

Advantages of Group Decision

Although a study of the principles and factors involved in group dynamics is a rewarding experience, if undertaken seriously, it is not our purpose here to go into this rather specialized area.[4] We simply want to point out some advantages that group discussion, group decision, and group action have over the practice of leaving the individual to make his decision alone.

Some objections met. There are teachers who say, "I just teach the spiritual truth and let the class members make their own application because I don't know what their particular needs are." Such an admission on the part of the teacher is no justification for ineffective teaching nor does it invalidate the principle that is here being suggested. It is the responsibility of the teacher to know the individual class members well enough to know what their particular needs are.

---

4. For those who are interested in the study of group dynamics we suggest the following as good, popular treatments of the subject: Wittenberg, *The Art of Group Discipline*; Wittenberg, *So You Want to Help People.*

Other teachers say, "I teach the general truth because my class members need different things. When I teach the truth in general terms, each member is left free to make his own application." It is true that the class members will have needs that differ, but this simply indicates that it is the teacher's responsibility to adapt the spiritual teaching according to the differing needs of each individual.

Another teacher may say, "I don't want to be too personal." This is a valid consideration on the part of the teacher that must be faced. When a teacher leads the group to analyze and evaluate their present experience in light of some spiritual ideal, the discussion undoubtedly is getting personal. The teacher may feel that this kind of teaching is too personal and that the class members will resent it.

Three things need to be said. First, it would depend upon the attitude and spirit of the teacher as to whether the class members would object to this kind of teaching. If the teacher has built up the proper relationship between himself and his class members, if he demonstrates a sympathetic attitude toward the problems and viewpoints of all the class members, and if the class members understand and appreciate the approach of the teacher, they will welcome rather than resent such teaching.

In the second place, he must use common sense in this type of teaching. He must recognize where his members are in relation to a given Christian attitude and lead them step by step toward the ideal. He should not try to lead them to take too long a step at any one time. Insofar as is possible, the teacher should deal with problems objectively rather than subjectively and personally.

In the third place, it must be admitted that there are probably some individuals who would resent having Sunday school teaching become this personal. They would rather come to a class where the Bible truth is taught and their lives are not bothered. There are people who will accept everything that Christianity teaches so long as it does not affect or change their way of living. But when Christianity makes demands that would necessitate changes, they get their feelings hurt and stop coming to church. In answering this objection, the teacher must decide for himself whether his task is to rock people to sleep or to seek to lead them to grow in the likeness of Christ.

A positive view. As a general rule people are more willing to make a change as a member of a group rather than as an individual.

Findley B. Edge

When an individual is left alone to make his own decision, he misses the benefit of the thinking of the group. He does not know about the victories that have been won by other members of the class in the particular area that is being considered. He does not know of the struggles and difficulties that others have faced and overcome with regard to a given course of action. As a result of missing all of this, he feels that he is the only one who faces this problem, and he tends to rationalize his position and continue in his present attitude.

On the other hand, as a member of the group he has the benefit of group thinking and group discussion. He hears and evaluates the ideas and points of view of others. In hearing of their problems, their struggles, their victories, the individual is strengthened and encouraged to do what he knows he ought to do.

In the second place, to follow a given course of action as a member of a group becomes an adventure and a challenge. A class of young adults may decide to do something about the "joint" that is on the corner two blocks from the church. One alone would not think of doing anything about it, but the same individual, as a member of a group, would consider this course of action a real challenge to his Christianity.

As a member of a group the individual has group support. If, with the group, he engages in a course of action that is unusual; if for example, he undertakes to fight some flagrant in the community, he does not feel that he is being fanatical. He is not the only one "sticking his neck out" when he works with a group. He is willing to do things as a member of the group that he would never have the courage to do alone.

There is no guarantee that if a teacher will follow this plan carry-over will take place. It is simply that a teacher, using this plan, will have a better chance to secure carry-over in the lives of class members than he would if he followed the plan of making a general application.

4

Lois E. LeBar
Education That Is Christian (1958)

The divine Teacher, with the cooperation of the human teacher, leads the pupil from his current need into the Word, where he gains new insight into truth, then out again to practice the Word in daily life situations.

Lois E. LeBar

About Lois E. LeBar

Lois Emogene LeBar (1907–1998) was born in Olean, New York. She attended a Methodist church as a child. While rooted in the evangelical religious education tradition, LeBar was also influenced by progressive educators. For example, she studied with William Heard Kilpatrick, a disciple of John Dewey. His emphasis on student interest, motivation, and purposeful activity seemed to operationalize much of what LeBar believed. She also developed an interest in John Amos Comenius. For LeBar, Comenius seemed to incorporate the best progressivism, minus the relativism and anti-supernaturalism of philosophical pragmatism.[1] Harold Burgess writes, "She seems to have been more aware of the teaching-learning process than were her evangelical contemporaries during the period of her greatest influence, the 1950s and 1960s."[2]

LeBar taught at Moody Bible Institute (1935–1942), but spent most of her professional life at Wheaton College (1945–1975). During this long tenure, she influences a great number of future evangelical Christian educators. LeBar served as review editor for *Christian Life* magazine, and more significantly, was a founding leader of the Commission on Christian Education (Professors' Section) of the National Sunday School Association, the forerunner of the North American Professors of Christian Education (NAPCE).[3]

About Education That Is Christian

David P. Setran states that LeBar wrote *Education That Is Christian* in "response to the poor teaching she witnessed in her many visits to local churches. Her observations of hundreds of evangelical Sunday school programs had revealed both lifeless teaching and content unrelated to the lives of students."[4] She even names a chapter, "Teaching That Is Only Poor Lay Preaching."[5] LeBar explains that both the

1. Setran, "Lois E. LeBar."
2. Burgess, *Models*, 152.
3. Setran, "Lois E. LeBar."
4. Ibid.
5. LeBar, *Education That Is Christian*, 20.

Bible/content-centered approach used in traditional settings and the life-experience-centered approach used in secular/liberal settings are unhelpful. For Lebar, the curriculum should emphasize the living Word (Christ) and the written Word (Bible) as the center of Christian curriculum.[6] *Education That Is Christian* serves as a philosophical and methodological source that is both scholarly and practical.

Selected Text:
"Structuring the Curriculum"[7]

The transition from Scriptural foundations to actual teaching practice is bridged by the curriculum. Scriptural principles are implemented by the outlining of cycles and series of lessons, which are broken up into individual lessons. The word "curriculum" literally means a "racecourse." Traditionally the course was considered the *body of content* that the student covered in his educational progress. More recently the term connotes the *activity of the student* as he runs through various experiences which involve content.

In a Scriptural orientation the "curriculum" may be defined as those activities in relation to authoritative content that are guided or employed by Christian leadership in order to bring pupils one step nearer to maturity in Christ. These activities imply interaction of both teachers and pupils with the Word of God. Because learning, as previously defined, is an active, inner, on-going, disciplined process, the teacher does nothing that the pupils can more profitably do themselves.

The Center of the Curriculum

The most crucial question in structuring a curriculum is the question of its center. Do not all Christians agree that both authoritative content and personal experience are essential if pupils are to appropriate for themselves the full salvation that is offered to them in Christ? Neither factor of the curriculum, content, or experience,

---

6. Burgess, *Models*, 169; see also LeBar, *Education*, 203–7.
7. Ch. 8 in LeBar, *Education*.

can be omitted or minimized with impunity. But one of them must constitute the center around which the other revolves, the source of authority upon which the other depends as a secondary element.

In poor traditional Christian education the content of the Bible was the whole curriculum. Bible facts were diligently studied by the teacher and given out to pupils, who were expected to absorb them mentally, to memorize them, and then automatically to apply them. The experience which resulted from the teaching of these facts was haphazard. Sometimes pupils were sufficiently motivated to practice them, sometimes they saw the relationship between these facts and their own daily lives, but these connections between the Bible and life were not an integral part of the lesson. Sometimes also the pupils got through the printed words on paper and the factual data of Scripture to have personal dealings with the Lord, but often they did not. Many are the young people who have been exposed to enough factual Scripture to enable them to live deeply spiritual lives, yet they have not actively inwardly appropriated the truth that they understand mentally.

At the other extreme is the secular and religious liberal curriculum that is centered in experience. Since it is the pupil who must do the growing, who must accept the content, he is given priority in the school's activities. As the pupils' needs are met, as they are motivated to interact with content that meets their needs, they originate and reorganize relevant content and bring it to life. The advocates of experience-centered systems assert that no curriculum that is centered in content can be dynamic, only the ones that are centered in life. Only as pupils search and find the content that has a bearing on current life will it enrich and change life.

What is the truth in this outlook? What the weakness? Can Christians accomplish their aims in a structure that is man-centered? No, only a God-centered curriculum can be Christian. Can we put the Word of God in the center and yet have a dynamic curriculum? We can, for no other book is comparable to God's Revelation. God means His words to be more than facts, even eternal facts. He means them to reveal Himself and His Son. He never meant us to separate the written Word from the Living Word. The Living Word is contacted only through the written record. Therefore Christians have a curriculum that is Word-centered rather than Bible-centered.

And lo, what an amazing thing we have now! A curriculum that is centered not in sinful human life, but in divine Life Himself, eternal life, fullness of life, the Living Word revealed by the written Word! What center can compare with that for vitality and power!

But experience with the Word cannot be left to chance. It will not automatically proceed from the written Word. Teachers must make definite provision for including experience in the curriculum. Though not the center of the Christian structure, experience is necessary because:

> The aim of Christian education is maturity in Christ to the glory of God.
>
> The Word must be personally, actively appropriated.
>
> Knowledge alone is not power, but the effective use of knowledge.
>
> Experience is the best teacher if it is guided by the Word.
>
> Factual content alone is only theory, sterile verbalism.

Therefore experience occupies an essential though secondary place in the Christian curriculum. The Word of God is originally an outer factor, external to the learning pupil. But as the divine and human teachers stimulate interaction between the Word and the pupil, both written and Living Word gradually or suddenly penetrate to the interior of the pupil. It is the peculiar ministry of the Holy Spirit to make the outer Word an inner experience, for He operates both without and within. As the outer Word becomes experience, there is progressively less of the self-life and more of the Christ-life until the Lord Himself becomes the controlling factor in the whole of life. Maturity in Christ consists of the Word's becoming our experience, becoming our life.

The divine Teacher, with the cooperation of the human teacher, leads the pupil from his current need into the Word, where he gains new insight into truth, then out again to practice the Word in daily life situations. The pupil's experience impels him to seek knowledge of the Word, which in turn commands him to return to life to practice the truth. The real test is the amalgamation of inner and outer forces until it is difficult to separate them. The Word becomes flesh, and our mortal bodies reflect the Word. How tremendous would be the results if all Bible teaching would set in motion these earth-shaking forces!

Developing a Unit of Work

Whenever a new series of lessons is projected or a series in current use fails to meet specific needs, how do teachers or writers proceed to set up the type of interaction that has just been described? All leaders need to understand curriculum structure, for they will use it even in adapting printed materials, and who does not need to do that? Who can expect to find ready-prepared lessons that are tailored to fit individual groups? Major publishing houses must meet typical needs, and whose needs are typical?

When all the principles discussed in this book are brought to bear upon the problems of curriculum, the result is a unit of work. The ministry of Christ on earth may be divided into two main curriculum units: the early part of His life up to Peter's confession of His deity, which was the culminating activity of the first unit; then the latter part of His life culminating in His death, resurrection, and ascension. The focal problem of the first unit is "Who am I?" Of the second, "What did I come to do?" The events within these two major units naturally fall into minor units, some of which are most naturally expressed in terms of content, as "the nature of the Kingdom"; and some in terms of experience, as "faith."

A unit of work may be defined as the organization of teaching-learning situations around a central core, a focal problem, that integrates both content and experience for the learner. A unit may be a long-term project lasting a year or two, or a short-term project consisting of three or four lessons.

There are many reasons for organizing curriculum materials into units of work. Units emphasize learning rather than teaching, thus stimulating new pupil experiences with content when it is more natural for teachers to stress content at the expense of experience. Units afford continuity both of content and experience. Especially in Christian agencies which hold sessions lasting only one hour a week, with seven days between, is it difficult for pupils to appreciate the relationship between separate lessons. If long-range goals are sighted and plans are made for reaching them, each discrete activity is seen in the light of the whole rather than as a fragmentary bit. Then motivation is stronger, integration surer. It is easier for both teachers and pupils to be flexible in revising plans to keep up with changing needs. When the content is connected with current life, it is either used or made ready to use as an integral part of the unit.

It is not to be expected that units of work developed for one agency will take the same form as those developed for other agencies. For instance, the curriculum outlined for Sunday school, one hour a week, looks quite different from a camping curriculum that runs every hour, consecutively, for two weeks. Likewise, a curriculum planned for young children who cannot read and who have little foresight will appear quite different from one planned for young people who can do independent research and committee work. What does remain the same under all circumstances is the underlying spirit of a unit of work, the spirit of quest and adventure and discovery, in which pupils seek and find new things in the Lord, in which they identify their own needs and meet them in Christ.

The Teacher's Preplanning

Putting emphasis on the pupils' learning rather than the teacher's teaching doesn't mean that we teachers are less important or that we'll have less to do. It probably means that we'll have more to do. As followers of John Amos Comenius, who first enunciated this emphasis, we plan and prepare in relation to our pupils as well as our content. We must experientially know both pupils and content. Formerly content was sufficient.

First we pray through and study thoroughly the needs, interests, capacities of our particular group in the light of the Word of God. On the basis of these needs we formulate general and specific aims. The general aims we keep in the back of our minds, glad when we see gradual progress along those lines. The specific aims we keep written large upon our hearts, relating everything that happens to them. If possible, the outstanding objective should be stated in a single, short sentence or phrase so that our focus is not blurred. This aim is best stated in terms of new conduct, attitudes, skill or knowledge, often in terms of a change in conduct which also involves attitudes, skills and knowledge.

We then select general and specific areas of essential content that meet these needs. The needs will be met by the written Word of God which leads to the Living Word, but not by just any part of the written Word. Teachers ought to be ready to suggest that part of the Bible that is closest to the problematical life situation, whose characters have most in common with our life today. James 1:21 uses the figure of the engrafted Word, the inserting of a fruitful shoot into wild natural stock until a permanent union is effected. The closer the Scripture is to life today, the easier will be the union.

Next we saturate ourselves with this part of God's Word until we are wholly absorbed with it. Until we feel it, breathe it, live it, dream it. Until we are completely at home with its implications. Until we are so filled with its possibilities for our own class that we are bursting to do something about it. Then we are ready to lead our pupils to that same vision and action. Then we can be free and flexible in our use of this eternal truth with pupils who are full of surprises.

The next step is to visualize various types of intrinsic motivation. Probably the most important single factor in the success of a unit of work is the enthusiasm with which it is launched. If it gets off to a running start, this push-off gathers enough momentum to carry it a long way. Otherwise feet will drag and interest lag. Even if an adequate launching should take a whole hour or more, it is time well spent, for the planning in itself is an educational experience. Planning requires the selection of past experience and content, insight into relationships between past and future, judgment as to possible procedures.

In terms of all we know and can discover about the members of our group, we find the points where the content areas touch their current lives and make a difference in what they want to do here and now. What is the connection between their felt needs and God's answers? It may be that we'll need to lead into their real spiritual needs as a second step rather than the first, if to begin there would leave them cold. No matter how far away from the final goal we have to start, the take-off must be where they are right now or they won't move toward the goal. It won't help them at all for us leaders to take the trip without them. It must be their unit, their progress, their values, their work.

Intrinsic motivation taps the pupils' inner drives and urges that the Lord God has put within all of us. It holds out something that is worth knowing and doing for its own sake. Even if the present level of motivation is rather low because higher levels as yet hold no appeal, even if the pupils *see* no connection between spiritual standards and their own daily life, still we must get them in touch with spiritual Reality at a low level rather than train them to seek selfish ends.

Extrinsic motivation implies that spiritual life is not worth seeking for its own sake. It holds out to pupils irrelevant prizes or rewards that have nothing to do with the major thrust of the unit. It implies that studying the Bible is an unpleasant task which requires sugar-coating to make it palatable. Nothing is more important in the Christian life than motives. We want our young people to desire the Lord first of all for Himself—nothing is more attractive than He is—and to desire the things of the Lord because they satisfy the inmost longings of the soul. They must experience the joy of fellowship with Him before He can trust them with His gifts or His service.

Therefore we'll bestir ourselves to create a setting which will arouse thought and questions along the line of the unit. For children this setting may be effected by large objects that they can manipulate, pictures that they can discuss, trips that afford new experience. For young people and adults we can steer informal conversation to questions in a given area, we can write thought-provoking questions on the chalkboard, we can espouse experiments and new projects that they show interest in. The best leads are always those that arise naturally out of the pupils' daily grappling with their own daily life situations.

Planning with the Pupils

If a unit of work is to be the pupils' rather than the teacher's, if they are to become actively involved so that they do the learning, they must share in the planning. If we leaders have previously prepared ourselves to lead them, they won't flounder and waste time, for we have already envisaged some of the possibilities that will work and some that won't be practical. But if we are true leaders rather than dictators, we're ready to let go our plans if the pupils come up with something better. They may prefer to adopt a plan we have conceived rather than anything they originate. That is perfectly legitimate, just so they wholeheartedly accept it.

But they must shoulder the problem. If they feel that it is ours rather than theirs, they'll let us carry it, and then we'll get the benefit, not they. Only if it is their problem, will they keep it on their hearts and assume responsibility for its solution.

It is often practical to write on a chalkboard what the pupils already know about the problem, and what they would like to find out. These areas are then organized and broken up into sub-problems, and the order of attack decided upon. It may be that the whole group will want to work on the whole problem, or the group may divide into committees that each take one aspect. If committees are used, it is well to have a natural leader in each group.

The main purpose and subsidiary purposes should be clarified very specifically so that the pupils know exactly what they're looking for in God's Word and just how they will go about it. This planning should be much more detailed than it usually is.

It is not to be assumed that this initial planning will be followed rigidly to the end of the unit. As the group gets into the content, new insight and new background will often necessitate a change of plans if real needs are to be met. Continual evaluation is an integral part of the process. At intervals the students pause to see how far they have come, and to r

evise plans for the future. As the teacher helps them solve their felt needs, he tries to go on to help them sense and meet their real spiritual needs.

Finding the Answers

If the problems are the pupils' own and they see clearly how to attack them, they will be ready to mobilize their energies in finding the answers. Many types of activity will be included in most units, most of them requiring thought and judgment rather than listening and rote memorization. The pupils will continually be selecting content that is relevant to their problem, judging its value, organizing data, finding new leads, sharing their findings with others, evaluating the validity of their conclusions, and checking results. The genuine personal satisfaction they derive from reaching the solution is their best reward. They will be more ready to practice truth that they themselves have discovered.

As the pupils work, the teacher supervises, providing further motivation should interest lag, suggesting new approaches or sources, helping to organize and evaluate what is found. The teacher's business is to keep the pupils working profitably and to help them appreciate the significance of what they find.

Of course the first specific method is always research in Scripture for pupils who can read, listening to a Bible story for those who cannot read. Young people need to realize that the answers to their practical questions are found in Scripture if they only know where to look and how to translate Hebrew customs and problems in terms of current living. The teacher guides them in making concrete factual observations of what the Bible actually says before they try to interpret what it means for them. They form the habit of depending upon the illumination of the Holy Spirit, of comparing Scripture with Scripture, of sharpening their intellectual perception.

Supplementing Bible study will be the use of versions, concordances, Bible dictionaries, atlases, commentaries, notes on manners and customs, and pictures. In order to learn how biblical principles are implemented in our day, the pupils may interview the Lord's people, make surveys, send questionnaires, write letters, visit churches and missions and museums, study architecture, make collections, illustrate Scripture and hymns. Whenever possible, direct experience should be substituted for vicarious experience with words.

The teacher should be flexible enough to substitute another phase of essential content for the one he had planned in order to meet each response as it arises, but should do this without disrupting the overall curriculum. If he feels led, or time and circumstances do not permit pupil activity, he does not hesitate to give direct instruction that meets the needs.

Lois E. LeBar

Culminating Activity

A curriculum unit is brought to the most satisfying conclusion when some type of activity ties the whole process together and if possible makes use of the main findings. Every curriculum should end in practice of the truth, or at least in visualization of the difference that truth ought to make in daily life. Unless our pupils can use the new truth in new situations, it is not really their own, and they will soon forget it.

A common example of culminating activity is the closing demonstration of a Vacation Bible School when the pupils share with their parents and friends what they've been doing during the school. This program introduces nothing new and extraneous, but selects the most interesting things from the regular schedule. If the demonstration includes spiritual progress as well as factual material, it can be of great value to the pupils themselves as well as to their guests. It sharply focuses the main purpose of the school and aids the transfer of Scripture to daily life.

The culminating activity may take a variety of forms. One may be the organization of findings into a chart or outline or time line. Since all groups need organization of content insofar as the age level is able to appreciate it, the whole should be viewed at the end as well as at the beginning. In a functional review the main thrust of a unit stands out more clearly, with the significance of each part seen in relation to the whole. The best way to review is to use.

If committees are working on several aspects of a problem, they may plan interesting ways of presenting their reports to the other groups, and then all may formulate a summary of the whole. If group members have gained new insights into spiritual life, they may use them to lead a worship service for another group. They may show what they have gained by constructing a work of art or a mural or a model, or by the creative writing of a magazine article, a letter, a report to the church, a story, tract, or skit. Some units are of such a nature that their natural outgrowth is a service project, such as building a playground for children, decorating a room at church, collecting papers to sell, weeding a garden, or putting on a banquet in appreciation for the work of others.

During all the steps of a curriculum unit the teacher should keep on the lookout for leading-on values. Does this study motivate the group to study a related question? Did relevant questions arise that could not be incorporated into this unit, but which the group showed real enthusiasm for? When once our Bible teaching comes to grips with real life as it is being currently lived, we won't need artificial stimulation; we'll be alert to new needs as they arise and start our teaching there.

An Example of a Curriculum Unit

For a brief illustration of a unit of work, let's take a series of Sunday school lessons on the subject of the Holy Spirit for Junior High young people. We as teachers open a new manual to the first unit of five lessons:

> The Holy Spirit as Teacher and Guide
> The Holy Spirit as Counselor
> The Holy Spirit as Illuminator
> The Holy Spirit as Enabler
> The Holy Spirit as Convicter

First we survey the work for the whole quarter, and the place of this unit in the whole. We ask ourselves whether or not our particular class needs this emphasis, and we immediately answer with assurance, "It surely does." Therefore we bow before the Lord with the names of our pupils on our hearts, asking Him to do His gracious inner work in each one, listing the specific things that need to be done in each life in relation to the Holy Spirit. "Dear Lord, help Jack to see that Thou art real, that Thou dost seek to speak personally to him by Thy Spirit through the Word, that Thou canst answer his doubts and fears." "Help Joan to find Thee as her best Pal, who can supply her emotional needs by Thy Spirit, and stabilize her life."

We then concentrate on the Scriptures that describe the person and work of the Holy Spirit until they have become so much a part of our thinking that we can turn readily from one passage to another. We apply all that we study to ourselves and ask the Spirit to give us new experiences with the Word. We also ask our divine indwelling Teacher to show us how the content of these five lessons can meet the specific needs of the class. Which part of this unit is closest to Jack's needs? Which to Joan's? As we study we are prompted by that same Holy Spirit to pray again that these truths may penetrate deep into consciousness and do a searching work in each life.

But we've been thinking of this new unit even before we make definite preparation to teach it. Even last quarter we were looking ahead in order to motivate it. When reference to God's Spirit was made in the study of the last topic, we took a minute to ask a few personal questions about the Holy Spirit. If the group responded by commenting or asking further questions, we'd pause to whet its appetite for this study, remarking that we ought to have a study of the Spirit in the future.

When the young people enter their classroom on the first day of the new unit, they find written on the chalkboard these questions:

> Do you know a Christian who is filled with the Spirit of God?
>
> Why do you think he is?
>
> Is the Spirit-filled Christian long-faced and serious?
>
> Is there anything spooky connected with the Spirit?
>
> Are young people ever filled with the Spirit? If so, do they die young?
>
> What questions do you have about the Spirit?

These very frank questions will undoubtedly get the group thinking about the subject as soon as they arrive. If you are there early, ready to use their comments, you can stimulate further questions that reveal individual concerns. You can write their questions on another chalkboard panel, and on still another write what they already know about the Holy Spirit. They will surely be bored if you begin to teach what they already know. But they'll be alert to discover the answers to their own questions.

If you have studied all five lessons in the series, you won't need to begin with the first one, or to keep arbitrary lines between the various ministries of the Spirit. You'll be able to. Begin with whichever problem seems most urgent and most introductory for your particular pupils as the Spirit enables you to sense their needs. You can begin at once to help them find their answers in Scripture and to discuss the practical implications to their own lives. You won't need to *tell* them the answers because they'll be turning the pages of their Bibles until they locate a passage that speaks to them personally. If they have prepared an assignment for today, that background will facilitate the search for answers to these new questions. You will act as stimulator and guide to make sure they see valid relationships and interpretations. The class period will find the pupils busily engaged in exploring their own Bibles and making their own applications.

The next four Sundays will be a continuation of this teaching-learning process. Each session will normally raise as well as answer several questions about the Holy Spirit. At the end of each session the pupils should have a personal problem to study and pray about during the week, a practical problem dealing with what the Spirit seeks to do in their lives or just how He can help them.

Each week when they leave class they should also have one definite truth in relation to the Spirit to act upon during the week. It might be His wisdom in difficult decisions, it might be His power in avoiding temptation and overcoming self, it might be His conviction of sin as they pray for a loved one. In pre-session the following Sunday they are encouraged to discuss how the Spirit aided them during, the week. This discussion will keep the study realistic and down to earth.

Another way to demonstrate the dynamic reality of the Spirit today is to suggest that young people interview mature respected members of the church who radiate the fullness of Christ. They may like to ask how the Holy Spirit operates under certain conditions that they are curious about. Advanced pupils may like to read and report on parts of books that describe how the Spirit moved young people like Hudson Taylor of the China Inland Mission and William Borden of Yale. Assuredly the presence of the Spirit should be felt in the group as He supplies the teacher with supernatural insight and enables the pupils to appropriate the Word.

Near the end of the unit the teacher is watching for cues that would lead to a profitable culminating activity. If Joan remarks that her sister needs the help of the Holy Spirit, the teacher might comment that the class could plan and conduct a worship service when they could share with Joan's sisters class the impact of what they have been learning. If the pastor of another evangelical church in town happens to be preaching Sunday evening on this subject, they might attend in a group and enjoy a snack at Teacher's house afterward. They might like to summarize their study by making a list of Bible references that would help them when they don't know what decision to make, when they feel discouraged, when they feel lonely, etc. Some groups enjoy making a list of fallacies about the Holy Spirit and posting it on the church bulletin board. If we teachers are sensitive to cues that the pupils give, and if we habitually make the most of such suggestions, they will often propose good ideas themselves.

Criteria for Evaluating Materials

Since a rare combination of insight and skill is required before a teacher is qualified to prepare his own Bible lessons, most of us are glad to leave that task to experts who are professionally trained. But each church is responsible for selecting the series of lessons that comes closest to meeting its local needs. Sad to say, the selection is often made on the basis of how easy the lessons are to teach or how colorful the jacket is.

What teachers should look for in printed manuals is the extent to which the writers help them apply Scriptural principles to the local situation. Local teachers in all kinds of schools in all parts of the country need material that achieves a delicate balance between specificity and flexibility. If suggestions are not definite and practical, teachers fail to get clear-cut ideas of teaching procedures, for generalizations and abstractions are not readily translated into action. If suggestions are not flexible, teachers are inclined to follow the manual slavishly without making connections with their own classes.

The Scriptural principles explained in this book work out in the following criteria for evaluating printed materials:

I. Use of Content

    A. Is the Bible regarded as the objective, propositional Word of God, the infallible guide to faith and practice, the source of authority?

    B. Is the curriculum centered in the Word of God—the written record revealing the Living Word?

C. Does the content emphasize biblical essentials: regeneration, growth in grace, service?

D. Are the biblical facts used in an accurate and forceful manner?

E. Is the extra biblical content true to Scriptural principles and introduced for the purpose of making the Bible relevant to daily life?

F. Is the whole curriculum unified and comprehensive, with each part properly integrated in the whole? It is comprehensive if it attains the nine ultimate aims of Christian education: right relation to God the Father, Son, the Holy Spirit; knowledge and love and practical use of the Bible; formulation of a Christian world and life view; a progressively closer walk with Christ; assuming of responsibility in the church, for the lost everywhere, and in the civic community.

II. Use of Experience

A. Is the individual helped to grow continually and to take definite steps toward balanced maturity in Christ?

B. Is provision made for major and minor decisions so that the pupils develop their own personal convictions?

C. Is provision made for pupil purposing, the solution of vital problems, and the carrying out of ideas?

D. Are the pupils' personal, immediate experiences used whenever possible rather than vicarious experiences?

E. Does the curriculum stress the essential elements in the pupils' experience and minimize the less essential (spiritual progress primarily; mental, psychological, social, physical, secondarily)?

III. Relation of Content and Experience

A. Is the Bible used functionally to produce changes in pupils rather than as an end in itself?

B. Is the material selected and graded to meet the present interests, needs, and capacities of the average pupil at the various age levels?

C. Does the curriculum make provision for meeting the needs of home, church, secular school, and community?

IV. IV. Meeting the Needs of the Pupil

A. Does the material appeal to and challenge the individual?

B. In the activities suggested for pupils, is provision made for individual differences—between pupils, classes, geographical areas, etc.?

C. Are the psychological needs of the individual met: freedom from guilt, security, affection, recognition, new experiences?

V. Meeting the Needs of the Teacher

A. Is the material self-explanatory, practical, definite?

B. Is the material flexible enough to meet the needs of large and small churches, trained and untrained teachers, pupils with diverse backgrounds, diverse

C. geographical areas?

D. Is the general tone of the material one of spiritual warmth, vitality, challenge?

E. Does the curriculum provide inspiration, biblical background, and teaching principles in addition to definite suggestions for lessons?

F. Does it guide the teacher in using life situations of his own pupils to make the Bible real to them?

VI. Meeting the Needs of the Agency

A. A. Does the curriculum take advantage of the distinctive needs and possibilities of the agency for which it is prepared? (For the Sunday school: primarily instruction and worship; for the Vacation Bible School: all four elements of instruction, worship, expression, fellowship; etc.)

B. Mechanical Features of Printed Materials

C. Do the high quality and standards of the material reflect its eternal values?

D. Is the material printed in a manner that facilitates teaching and learning: layout, type, binding, vocabulary, illustrations?

Using Printed Lesson Materials

Even after a school has selected the series of lessons that comes closest to meeting its particular needs, it must expect to adapt that series to local conditions. Not because the series has weaknesses as printed curriculum, but of necessity it has to be written for typical teachers and typical pupils in typical situations. And those situations exist only in educational textbooks. This does not imply lack of respect for lesson writers, who should be professionally trained in age-group methods. The local teacher should try to find the reason why the manual suggests everything that is in it. Lesson writers have reasons that local groups aren't always aware of and that should be discovered before teachers dismiss them summarily as inappropriate.

But the most expert of writers can't write for any one church. Therefore teachers must know what in their manuals they should expect to adapt, and how. If teachers first of all sit before the Lord with the needs of their own pupils upon their hearts, they will be in a mood for picking up their manual and relating all they read to their own class. Nothing will take the place of preliminary prayer, which focuses the personal needs of the pupils in the light of the Father's best for them.

Long-Range Planning

A teacher should then read the whole manual, absorbing the perspective and flavor of the whole quarter. As he reads, he evaluates in terms of his own class. Does the spirit of the whole meet the needs of my pupils? Should they be different people after studying these lessons? Do the aims seem to be pointed directly at them—deeply, personally? Would a slight change of focus do more for them? Is each lesson needed by them, or is there one aspect of the whole that is most urgently needed? Can I strengthen this emphasis without destroying the continuity of the series? Might it be wise to revamp a lesson or two in order to stress the needed emphasis?

If a teacher has previewed the whole quarter, he will be able to teach pupils more flexibly within that framework. If a pupil is bothered today about a question that comes in a later lesson, it might be wise to take that lesson today rather than to put him off until later when he may have lost all interest in the subject. A pupil's readiness for a subject counts more than its logical organization, though that should follow if interest is retained. If we are ready to suggest Scripture that answers a pupil's question, we are often able to incorporate it into the day's lesson without switching subjects. Such is the richness of God's Word that a given passage often teaches more than one principle and may without distortion be approached from more than one angle.

Particularizing the Approach

When teachers read the lesson approach that is printed in their manual, they should ask themselves:

> Will this approach make my pupils sit on the edge of their chairs?
>
> Is this a problem with which they're vitally concerned?
>
> How much momentum will this approach gain for the lesson?

At times teachers will be satisfied that the approach suggested in the manual is the best possible beginning for the lesson. At other times the printed approach would no doubt leave a particular class cold.

Teachers will then ask themselves these questions as they conjure up in their mind's eye their own Harry and Ann:

> How can their personal world be tapped to lead into the Bible content?
>
> Where does this truth touch their daily lives?

What of consequence happened to them this very week? What may be on their minds and hearts as they come to Bible class?

The carrying power of the whole lesson will depend largely upon the approach. If the pupils get personally involved at the very beginning, they will normally search for answers, catch insights, offer suggestions, in general "push" the lesson. The process of visualizing various types of intrinsic motivation is the same as that for motivating a unit of work, which was analyzed earlier in this chapter. If more than one approach is sighted, it is easier for the teacher to discard them in favor of one that the pupils offer spontaneously at the moment, for the latter will no doubt gather up most force.

Using the Pupils' Interaction

After the approach gets the pupils initially involved, the methods used should keep them continually interacting with the Word of God, written and Living. We are not truly teaching when we lecture content regardless of what the pupils are doing and thinking. It is their interaction that determines how we proceed. They must progressively receive more and more of the written Word, which will lead them to receive more and more of the Living Word. As they themselves discover the exciting truths of the eternal world, it becomes easier for them to obey those truths.

If children have heard the day's story given in the manual, we don't proceed to tell it anyway and thereby to bore them and engender negative attitudes toward Scripture. Perhaps we ask them to tell it, or parts of it. Or read it directly from their Bibles, if they are able. When they begin to tell it, they may discover that there are many details that they don't know; then they'll be ready to look or listen for them.

In an atmosphere that encourages questions and comments and suggestions, we follow through every honest contribution. If members of the group frown or look puzzled, we find out what is behind that facial expression. If a sudden insight is gained, we may be able to spurt ahead and cover more material than is scheduled for one lesson. If pupils are not ready for a truth because they lack background, we may have to back up, add supplementary material, and slow down.

When someone asks a question that seems irrelevant, we try to discover what connection the ideas had in his mind, which may be just the clue that will open up his life to the glorious Light of the world. (That is, unless he is being flippant and just trying to gain attention.) Often we must look beneath the question to the questioner, for timid souls ask factual questions to hide the real personal question that is lurking inside. It often happens that a pupil tries out the group until he finds whether or not he is accepted as a person in his own right, whether he is permitted to express what he actually feels, though it may appear heretical.

What do we do when pupils make comments such as:

> I don't believe that.
>
> Why do scholars disagree on this point?
>
> How can we find out what the Holy Spirit wants to do in each of us?
>
> How can I be my brother's keeper?
>
> I could draw a picture that shows what we've been talking about.
>
> Shouldn't we show this community that we are Christians?

Many earnest teachers never hear comments like this. Yet they are invaluable leads to the sensitive teacher, for every remark like these means that the pupils have been taking the Word unto themselves and are reacting to it. If they form the habit of making the Word personal and doing something about it, they are on their way to maturity in Christ. We don't know what they're thinking unless they tell us. We don't know how to proceed unless they show us where they are now. Why not encourage them to give illustrations of Scriptural principles instead of doing it ourselves? As pupils make suggestions for projects and activities, they will aggressively assume responsibility for carrying them out. The work will be theirs, the class theirs, the growth theirs.

Evangelical Christian Education

Providing Opportunities for Practice

If a teacher truly believes that ". . . to him that knoweth to do good and doeth it not, to him it is sin" (James 4:17), he will not consider his Bible lesson finished when the Scriptural principles have been discovered. He will not assume that pupils will automatically obey one of God's commands because they understand it mentally. Their whole being needs to be challenged in relation to that mental insight. Their wills and emotions are harnessed by means of worship, either a planned worship service, or spontaneous worship whenever emotional feeling reaches a high point, or a brief moment of worship at the culmination of Bible study. Instruction and worship then bring pupils to the place where they are prompted to do something outwardly about the truth that they have received inwardly. Personal application should be an integral part of each lesson.

In every classroom there are opportunities for the practice of God's Word if teachers only had eyes to see them. As children work and play with relevant objects and handwork materials and visual aids, many occasions arise for sharing and cooperating and showing love. When all of them naturally want the longest pencil with the best eraser, a child can be commended when he leaves it for someone else. When several children want to move the leading figure on the flannel graph board, they form the habit of giving in to others. They learn to take turns sitting beside their beloved teacher. When only one may perform an active service that they'd all like to do, they should connect their own selfish or unselfish acts with the Bible stories and verses that they are learning to repeat.

Young people, and adults too, can often work out the truth in their Bible classes. The over-talker will not monopolize the discussion if he projects himself into the situation of the shy member, who has problems too, who needs to be brought out of himself by others who are concerned about his spiritual growth as well as their own interests. How many adult classes practice the precept: "Let nothing be done through strife or vainglory; but in lowliness of mind let each esteem other better than themselves. Look not every man on this own things, but every man also on the things of others" (Philippians 2:3-4)?

If teachers realize that pupils often have insights and experiences to contribute, they'll be democratic rather than dictatorial in their leadership of the group. When decisions are in the offing, they'll seek the mind of the Spirit in the group rather than trying to push through their own preferences.

Of course it isn't possible to practice in the classroom many of the truths of God's Word, because it is intended for the whole of life. But at least teachers can help their pupils visualize how the Christ-life may be lived at home and school and in work and play. They can use some of the lesson period for discussion of practical implications rather than

spending the whole time on the exposition of new truth when what is already known is not being put to work. Many a Christian businessman in theory holds high moral principles that he is not putting into operation in his office or shop. He has never seen his business practices from the viewpoint of God or his employees. In a warm, personal setting he needs to see the needs of the other fellow, who looks at the office or shop from a different perspective.

If there isn't time for both an intensive study of the Word and its application, adult Bible classes sometimes decide to hold roundtable discussions in homes during the week or on Sunday afternoon. For instance, a like-minded circle of Christian parents find it fascinating to ponder such questions as:

> In what sense is father the head of the house?
>
> What questions should the family council decide?
>
> What constitutes Christian culture in the home?
>
> How can family altar meet the current needs of various ages?
>
> How can members of a family enjoy each other on family night at home?

Young people can spend the Sunday morning hour in the Bible, then use their Sunday evening young people's hour for discussion of its implications. Each group can decide how long and how often it wants to meet, just so this expressional part of the Christian program is not omitted.

Christians who get into the habit of being doers of the Word and not hearers only will continually be initiating group and individual projects. Why should not Christians be the first to lend a helping hand to a family in an emergency, when a home burns or when a mother is lost? When rooms in the church need redecorating, it should not be necessary to hire outsiders. If group members support wholly or partially a missionary known personally to them, they will find it harder to live in luxury and ease when their friends afar lack the necessities of life.

If our pupils begin to experience the thrill of seeing the Lord of life work through them, they'll be open to many urgent needs that will take them out of themselves and their own narrow lives.

5

Lawrence O. Richards
Creative Bible Teaching (1970)

For spiritual growth and reality in Christian experience, faith demands response in all the varied situations of human life.

Evangelical Christian Education

About Lawrence O. Richards

Lawrence O. Richards (1931–) was born in Milan, Michigan, and was raised in a Presbyterian household.[1] He was ordained at a nondenominational church in Dallas, Texas. With over two hundred works, translated into twenty-four languages, Richards is considered by some as the most prolific evangelical Christian education writer during the last half of the twentieth century.[2] "Richards has outlined the most comprehensive theory of Christian education by any evangelical writer of the 20th century."[3] Richards is critical of Christian education that requires learners to remain passive.[4] He served as professor at Wheaton College Graduate School (1965–1972). In 1972, he moved to Phoenix, Arizona, and dedicated himself to writing and speaking. Over time, he became more open to the social science/theological approach, but always remained faithful to his biblical/theological roots.[5]

About Creative Bible Teaching

Several of Richards books are standard texts in the field of evangelical Christian education, but his "Hook-Book-Look-Took" approach in *Creative Bible Teaching*, later revised and co-authored with Gary J. Bredfeldt, is one of the most widely used methods in Bible teaching classrooms. According to Phillip Sell, the "'Hook-Book-Look-Took' format for Bible teaching provides a solid template for effective communication of the Bible. It is particularly important because this format became the approach of almost all of the evangelical Sunday school curriculum publishers."[6]

---

1. Sell, "Lawrence O. Richards."
2. Ibid.
3. Ibid.
4. Burgess, *Models*, 156, 155.
5. Anthony and Benson, *Exploring*, 372.
6. Sell, "Lawrence O. Richards."

Lawrence O. Richards

Selected Text:
"The Pattern: HBLT Approach"[7]

Imagine boarding an airplane you know was designed without a plan. Or how about zooming up an elevator to the sixty-seventh floor of an urban skyscraper that was built without architectural drawings and plans. Frightening thought! Because of the risk to life and limb, haphazard approaches to airplane design or structural engineering are unwise. But even in the lesser things of life, planning seems to be a wise action that prudent people undertake. Whether we are making a dress or making investments, a well-thought-out plan is essential. Most human endeavors require planning. As a general principle, things done right are done with a plan. Generals need battle plans, coaches need game plans, and teachers need lesson plans. This chapter is about lesson planning. It is about doing things right when it comes to teaching the Bible.

Spontaneity has its place. Certainly it is a welcome aspect of a relationship between a husband and wife. When he brings home flowers just because he saw a person selling them on the street corner, that's a good kind of spontaneity. Or when the family pulls off at John's Rock Museum on its way through the Black Hills just out of curiosity and it turns out to be a highlight of the family vacation, that's another good kind of spontaneity. When a student in your adult Sunday school class tells openly and spontaneously her personal story of a life struggle that fittingly illustrates a point made in class, and as a result people open up and discussion becomes more meaningful—that too is a good kind of spontaneity. But ironically, in teaching the Bible, planning must be done for spontaneity to be meaningful. Otherwise "spontaneity" is more likely to be small talk. The wise teacher knows when to set aside his agenda and even his theme, but he also has a theme that can bring students back to look at the passage when the discussion turns to topics more suited for casual conversations outside class. He is open to teachable moments, but his class does not wander aimlessly in the name of spontaneity.

It is interesting how some equate spontaneity with the leading of the Holy Spirit. Planning is looked at as a human characteristic that hinders the work of God in a group. It is believed that God works in a

---

7. Ch. 9 in Richards and Bredfeldt, *Creative Bible Teaching*.

spontaneous, unpredictable way. Some believe that worship services and teaching sessions should be free-flowing and unplanned. They believe that God leads in spontaneous ways that cannot occur when an order of service or a lesson plan is followed. They come to class and simply trust God to lead them and the class concerning what to say and what applications to make. But spontaneity is not God's way of working in the vast majority of situations. Remember what Paul said in response to the Corinthian church, whose spontaneous approach to worship had gotten out of hand. He said, "For God is not a God of disorder but of peace . . . everything should be done in a fitting and orderly way" (1 Cor. 14: 33, 40).

It is God's nature to plan. In fact, we take personal encouragement in the midst of our life struggles from this truth. We rest on the fact that God is not haphazard. He has a sovereign plan for our lives. God designed His world by very exacting plans. He orders events by a master plan. And we as human beings made in His image have an innate tendency to make plans as well. We plan our days. We plan events. We plan travel. We plan our work. We plan our homes. We plan our lives. We plan worship services. We even try to plan our families. Should we not develop plans for teaching the Word of God as well?

A Plan for Teaching

There are numerous ways one could plan a classroom experience. We are going to look at one with you in this book. We call it the HBLT approach. That stands for Hook, Book, Look, and Took. Don't worry, we already know it's a bit corny, but that's why you will never forget it! It is an easy-to-remember approach to lesson preparation that, when followed, opens up the student to learning biblical truth and to making meaningful application of the truth in his or her life.

It is not a new approach. In fact, when Paul addressed the philosophers at the Areopagus on Athens's Mars Hill, his approach to teaching paralleled the lesson planning approach we'll present here. So pause now and read the account from Acts 17. What steps did Paul follow in teaching his audience?

While Paul was waiting for them in Athens, he was greatly distressed to see that the city was full of idols. . . . Paul then stood up in the meeting of the Areopagus and said: "Men of Athens! I see that in every way you are very religious. For as I walked around and looked carefully at your objects of worship, I even found an altar with this inscription: TO AN UNKNOWN GOD. Now what you worship as something unknown I am going to proclaim to you.

"The God who made the world and everything in it is the Lord of heaven and earth and does not live in temples built by hands. And he is not served by human hands, as if he needed anything, because he himself gives all men life and breath and everything else. From one man he made every nation of men, that they should inhabit the whole earth; and he determined the times set for them and the exact places where they should live. God did this so that men would seek him and perhaps reach out for him and find him, though he is not far from each one of us. For in him we live and move and have our being': As some of your own poets have said, 'We are his offspring.'

"Therefore since we are God's offspring, we should not think that the divine being is like gold or silver or stone—an image made by man's design and skill. In the past God overlooked such ignorance, but now he commands all people everywhere to repent. For he has set a day when he will judge the world with justice by the man he has appointed. He has given proof of this to all men by raising him from the dead."

A few men became followers of Paul and believed. Among them was Dionysius, a member of the Areopagus, also a woman named Damaris, and a number of others. (Acts 17:16, 22–31, 34)

We find Paul in Athens waiting for Silas and Timothy to join him. While he waits for his ministry companions he takes a stroll around the city. He becomes personally distressed by what he observes. It is a city filled with idols. It is a place utterly lost and in need of Christ. So many idols exist that one even bears the inscription: "To an unknown God." How does Paul approach a people that so desperately needs the truth of Christ?

After doing his observational needs assessment, Paul strategizes the best approach with this group. He begins teaching in his students' world. He starts where they live. He tells of his observations and he stimulates their interest. In particular, his statement "now what you worship as something unknown I am going to proclaim to you" is designed to stimulate curiosity while giving direction to his teaching. Surely his listeners' ears must have perked up at that point. He had them hooked! They were ready to listen to more.

His next step was to explore the truth with them. He told them that all persons are created by God and that each one longs for a relationship with Him. He also declared the truth that the resurrected Jesus Christ provides the means for that relationship.

After gaining attention and presenting his message, Paul helped his hearers identify a general implication for all persons. He said, "In the past God overlooked such ignorance, but now he commands all people everywhere to repent. For he has set a day when he will judge the world with justice by the man he has appointed."

Finally, it was time to respond. Paul's teaching ministry moved from general implications to personal application. We are not told exactly how Paul brought learners to this response. Possibly it was without prompting from Paul at all. But some did believe, and, of course, others did not. Application can go either way when we teach biblical truth. Some may respond by rejection. There are no guarantees that all will respond as we would like. The important point is that all are brought to the place of a response. The lesson must lead to the point of action, which indeed Paul's did.

The Four Elements of Your Lesson

Your teaching aim has been developed from a study of the passage to be taught. It spells out in a flexible way the response for which you are teaching. You have a dear idea where you want to go. Now it's time to design a lesson that will get there. Creative Bible teaching lesson plans are composed of four basic sections—the Hook, the Book, the Look, and the Took.

It's best to avoid thinking of these as mechanical steps. They're more like four parts of a continuous, systematic but exciting process.

Lawrence O. Richards

In class the students probably won't even notice passage from one part of the process to another. No part is marked by routine; each is full of opportunity for flexibility and interaction. Yet each of these parts in the process has its own—and essential—role. Let's look at the four in sequence.

The Hook

You have prepared the class. You've been gripped by the truth you're to teach. You've seen it work in your life. When you come to class, you're excited about the lesson. But your students aren't. They haven't had your experiences, and they aren't thinking about your lesson. They have their own problems. One adult may be worrying about a late income tax return. Another is thinking about the iron left out: *Now, did I turn it off, or didn't I?* Others are contemplating significant personal matters like lost jobs, broken relationships, or sick and dying loved ones. A teen may be replaying last night's game or nursing the tragedy of a rejected date. A child may be still fuming over a fight with her sister and the fact that she was punished and her sister wasn't. All differ, but each comes to class operating on his or her own wavelength. You must seek to entice them away from their private thoughts and share in this time of learning. And so you use the hook. Fishermen use it to get the fish out of the lake into the boat. You use it to bring your students into the Word of life.

There are several qualities of a good hook:

1. It gets attention.

"When Princes Diana lost her life, it seems the whole world felt her loss. Many people say she had finally found happiness after years of searching. Team up with a person near you, and in two minutes come up with a list of what most people think makes them happy," asked Pete Carson of his senior adult Sunday school class. Here's something everyone can do, a way in which all can take part. He has their attention. The hook is in. But getting attention isn't the only task of a good hook.

2. It surfaces a need.

All of us have needs in our lives. Many of these are right at the surface of our conscious lives; others are more hidden from view and less obvious to us or others. Maybe we are experiencing tension with a coworker or neighbor. Possibly the need is in the form of financial stress or chronic illness. Some have need for friendships and a sense of belonging. Others may face family problems and failing marriages. Then there is the need for encouragement or mutual support in Christian parenting. We want to be godly husbands and wives, mothers and fathers. Children face needs related to family, friends, or school. They have needs that include encouragement, attention, recognition, and acceptance. Adolescents face needs requiring understanding, decision-making guidance, building healthy relationships with the opposite sex; and developing a sense of identity.

When we design the hook, we should have the needs of our group in view. The needs assessment we did earlier should guide us in devising a hook that surfaces needs in the group in a non-threatening, thought-provoking manner. When students sense that the class is related to their needs, they are far more likely to participate in the activities of the class and in the learning process. This can be difficult because frequently students' perceived needs and their true needs differ. The teacher must work to open students' minds and hearts to the spiritual needs Scripture addresses.

3. It sets a goal.

We might call this the "direction step." The Hook must provide something to answer the question, "Why should I listen to this?" This is a fair question. If this lesson is going to be about something important to me, I want to pay attention. If it's an irrelevant recounting of dusty data, I do not. Students make that decision quickly. In just the first few words you speak, students tune in or tune out. That's why a hook must set direction for the class. The teacher must give students a reason for listening.

After Pete's students listed their ideas of typical sources of happiness, he showed that the writer of Philippians spoke of joy at a time when his life was far removed from anything we associate with happiness. He then made this statement: "Our goal today is to discover what gave Paul joy, when he had nothing that most people think makes them happy." By this statement he told his class why they should pay attention. All of us want joy. To discover its source the class would listen. He had earned the right to teach. When your students have no reason for learning, no reason that is important to them, you'll find it hard to hold them. But set a goal they want to reach, and they'll be with you. Sometimes students set their goals too low—most of us would prefer to avoid suffering rather than finding purpose in it, for example—so helping them see Scripture through the mind of Christ and set worthy learning goals is part of the teacher's task.

4. One more thing.

The hook should lead naturally into the Bible study. When Pete turned to Philippians, the class was under way. A good hook is one of the secrets of effective Bible teaching. When you capture interest, set a goal, and lead your students into the Word, you have a good start on a creative class.

The Book

In the Book section the teacher seeks to clarify the meaning of the passage being studied. In this part of the teaching-learning process, the teacher helps his students get—and understand—the biblical information. Many methods are available for this purpose. The teacher can use a participatory one, such as buzz groups and small group reports. Or he can use a teacher-centered method. A good lecture is the fastest way to cover content and make points. Or one can use charts, visuals, and so forth. Whatever the method, the purpose in this part of the lesson remains constant: to give biblical information and help students understand it.

Pete decided to have the class divide into small groups. He gave each group a set of questions to consider that helped explore the meaning of the passage. He gave one volunteer member of each group a blank overhead transparency along with a marker to record their findings. Each group was to review several references to joy in Philippians. Then the groups reconvened to share the result of their study. After the groups reported back, Pete summarized the comments and said, "Great, now let's put the message of Philippians into a single sentence." After a few tries the class had a single sentence that described the theme of Philippians. Pete had led the class in meaningfully and purposefully exploring the text. As a result, the class had a much better understanding of the overall message of the book. Not only had Pete laid the foundation for the next several classes on this book, but he had set the stage for an investigation of the implications of biblical joy in the lives of his students.

The Look

When the students understand what the Bible says, it's time to move to implications. Their knowledge must be tempered with "spiritual wisdom and understanding" (Col. 1:9). So the next step the teacher must plan for in the lesson preparation process involves guiding the class to discover and grasp the relationship of the truth just studied to daily living.

In the Book section of the class, Pete's students discovered that the sources of Christian joy are getting out the gospel, sacrificing self for others, and the Lord Himself. They learned this through the use of small group inquiry methods. In essence, they gained a head knowledge understanding of the passage. What they discovered together was true information about the nature of Christian joy. But they had not yet identified the implications of that information for Christian living. Pete had to lead the group a step further. Through the Look section, Pete guided the class in dealing with the essential question necessary to reveal life implications. He asked, "But what does this mean for the pattern of our daily lives?" This is the issue explored in the Look section of the teaching plan. Let's see how the Look section unfolded in Pete's class.

Pete recognized that his senior adult class was comprised of Christians with a wide range of life experiences to draw upon. He decided that he would tap that wealth of experience in the group by using a combination of a case study and probing questions to encourage the discovery of implications from the group's study of Philippians. Pete distributed a case study. Here is the case the class was to discuss.

> Bob and Peg Short are a retired couple living in the Midwest. Bob has been retired from his job with a major airline for nearly eight years. He has just turned seventy-three and is in moderately good health. But faces a debilitating condition that will worsen in the next two to three years to the point where Peg will not be able to care for him alone. So, with reluctance, they decided to move into a life-care retirement community. Both were unhappy with the decision to move but felt that it was the best thing to do in their situation. They dreaded giving up their home and moving into the cramped apartment, and they wondered if they could ever be happy there.

Pete asked the class to consider how the principles they had just learned together might apply to this couple's lives. After much discussion and telling of personal stories related to the case study, the class concluded that Bob and Peg should look at the move as a commissioning to a new mission field. They suggested that they would have opportunities to tell of their faith, minister to others, and deepen their dependence on Christ. In the process of discussing Bob and Peg's case, the students were exploring practical ways that the material covered in class could be related to daily living. Pete summarized their ideas on the overhead. The result: the class had gone the next step in the study of the Bible—they had identified implications for daily life.

The Took

But, like a vaccination, the Word of God is of no effect until we can say it "took." Response is required. Normally, response to teaching will take place outside of class, in weekday life. "Faith by itself, if it is not accompanied by action," the Bible says, "is dead" (James 2:17). For spiritual growth and reality in Christian experience, faith demands response in all the varied situations of human life.

In the Look section of the lesson the teacher encourages such response. The teacher leads the class members to pinpoint personal areas in which they could respond and helps them plan specific ways they *will* respond. Often we leave church full of good intentions. We'll be more loving that week, more dedicated. But because the resolution is vague, because we haven't gone beyond the generalization and implementation phase of learning to actually plan *how* we'll change, no change takes place. The creative Bible teacher knows this. The goal is transformed lives—change. Therefore, creative Bible teachers help students respond by leading them to see God's will and by helping them decide and plan to do it.

Pete did this by distributing postcards to his class. He asked everyone to write their name and address on one side of the card. On the other side he asked them to write down how they would apply the passage in the week ahead. He reminded the group of the implications they had discovered and then gave them time to think and write. He collected the cards. On Monday he dropped them in the mail so that everyone would have a reminder that arrived in their mailbox later in the week. The next Sunday, the class discussed how they did applying the class on joy to their own life situations.

A Trip through Time

Another way to understand the Hook, Book, Look, Took approach is to picture it as a teacher-led trip through time. Movement of the lesson proceeds from the present (Hook) to the past (Book), back to the present (Look), and into the future (Took). Figure 13 depicts the lesson structure in this way. The teacher's role is one of travel agent and tour guide. As travel agent, the teacher plans the journey. As tour guide, the teacher then leads the trip. But, always, the students are in view. They are the ones doing the traveling. They are full participants in the travel experience. Travel agents and tour guides have a purpose—to enable others to make the journey.

Lawrence O. Richards

Values of Lesson Structure

The ability to handle lesson structure is invaluable to the Bible teacher. The process we've described and the key words (Hook, Book, Look, Took) suggested to characterize its parts are tools for the teacher. These are practical tools with which to develop structuring ability. How can these tools be used?

As a guide to method choice. When you understand the purpose of each part of the teaching process, it's easy to select methods. Most books on methods are rather confusing. They talk of role play, of buzz groups, of brainstorming, of dozens of other techniques, and give rules for their successful use. But what should determine your choice of method is function, the job a method is to do in class.

This is how you should understand methodology. A method is simply an activity designed to hook students, to communicate information and meaning, to lead to insight, or to encourage response. The next section of this book talks about activities suited to these purposes for various age groups. But the main thing is this. *If you understand what you are trying to accomplish, you can select or invent an activity to accomplish it.* Master the parts of the lesson process, and method skill will follow.

To simplify lesson planning. Breaking down the process of creative Bible teaching into four parts simplifies lesson planning. It's easy for a teacher who understands the parts of the lesson to build a lesson or to find and correct weaknesses in printed lesson material. Planning is enhanced when some sort of template is followed. That is the advantage of the Hook, Book, Look, Took format.

One More Example

Models are a way many of us learn best. We have to see how something is done, and then we can follow the pattern ourselves. So let's consider one more lesson planning example. We'll see how Alex, the youth worker who leads an urban group of adolescents in a weekly Bible study, planned his lesson on Hebrews 10:19–25. Table 13 is a copy of Alex's lesson plan that shows how he designed the study. You will notice that he has identified his exegetical idea, pedagogical idea, and lesson aims on his lesson plan worksheet. Following this, his worksheet is divided into four sections where he has written his Hook, Book, Look, and Took plans. Through the lesson, Alex hopes to lead his group to establish a group covenant involving a commitment to meet regularly for prayer and mutual support.

Table 14 is a lesson planning worksheet designed to assist you in putting together your own lesson plan. It brings together all of what you have learned to this point in this book. It shows how you can use your understanding of the lesson preparation process to develop a teaching plan. At the top of the worksheet is a place to record the date, the location, and a filing reference for the plan. Use these for future reference. Next is a box to summarize information about the target group. Draw this information from your needs assessment study. Below that are places to indicate the passage being studied and any cross references you plan to use. Continuing down the worksheet you will find boxes to write out the exegetical idea, pedagogical idea, and lesson aims that we discussed in previous chapters. Following these is space for your Hook, Book, Look, and Took. Notice that the Book section is divided vertically so that you can include both your content outline and the methods you plan to use to teach that content. Finally, there is a place to record any evaluative insights you might have after you teach the class. These will help you if you ever teach the material again.

Look over Table 14. Use it to prepare your next teaching session. Review chapters 1 through 9 if you need to. Make sure that your Hook gets attention, sets a goal, and leads into the Bible. Plan the Book to communicate both information and meaning. Check the Look to be sure you guide your students to implications. Finally, construct a Took that will aid and encourage response. The next chapter will give you further help with the application side of teaching, but you already have the tools you need to plan your class!

Bibliography

Anthony, Michael J., and Warren S. Benson. *Exploring the History & Philosophy of Christian Education: Principles for the 21st Century.* Grand Rapids: Kregel, 2003.
Boettner, Loraine. *The Reformed Doctrine of Predestination.* Grand Rapids: Eerdmans, 1932.
Burgess, Harold W. *Models of Religious Education: Theory and Practice in Historical and Contemporary Perspective.* Wheaton, IL: BridgePoint, 1996.
"The Creator, The Creation." The Stony Brook School. Online: http://stonybrookschool.org/arts/creator-creation.
Dobbins, Gaines S. *How to Teach Young People and Adults in the Sunday School.* Nashville: Sunday School Board of the Southern Baptist Convention, 1930.
Eavey, Charles B. *Principles of Teaching for Christian Teachers.* Grand Rapids: Zondervan, 1940.
Fawcett, Cheryl L., and Jamie Thompson. "Frank E. Gaebelein." Christian Educators of the 20th Century. Talbot School of Theology, Biola University. Online: http://www.talbot.edu/ce20/educators/protestant/frank_gaebelein/.
Gaebelein, Frank E. *Christian Education in a Democracy: The Report of the N.A.E. Committee.* Oxford: Oxford University Press, 1951.
———. "Evangelicals and Social Action." *Journal of the Evangelical Theological Society* 25 (1982) 17–22.
Gaebelein, Frank E., and D. B. Lockerbie, editors. *The Christian, the Arts, and Truth: Regaining the Vision of Greatness.* Portland, OR: Multnomah, 1985.
General Education in a Free Society: Report of the Harvard Committee. Cambridge, MA: Harvard University Press, 1945.
Howlett, Walter M., editor. *Religion, the Dynamic of Education; A Symposium on Religious Education.* New York: Harper, 1929.
Jordan, David Starr. *The Call of the Twentieth Century: An Address to Young Men.* Boston: American Unitarian Association, 1903.
Lay, Robert F. "Charles B. Eavey." Christian Educators of the 20th Century. Talbot School of Theology, Biola University. Online: http://www.talbot.edu/ce20/educators/protestant/charles_eavey/.

Bibliography

LeBar, Lois E. *Education That Is Christian*. Westwood, NJ: Revell, 1958.
Raffety, W. Edward. *The Smaller Sunday School Makes Good*. Philadelphia: American Sunday School Union, 1927.
Rausch, David A. *Arno C. Gaebelein, 1861–1945: Irenic Fundamentalist and Scholar*. Studies in American Religion 10. Lewiston, NY: E. Mellen, 1983.
Richards, Lawrence O., and Gary Bredfeldt. *Creative Bible Teaching*. Rev. ed. Chicago: Moody, 1998.
Sell, Phillip W. "Lawrence O. Richards." Christian Educators of the 20th Century. Talbot School of Theology, Biola University. Online: http://www.talbot.edu/ce20/educators/protestant/lawrence_richards/.
Setran, David P. "Lois E. LeBar." Christian Educators of the 20th Century. Talbot School of Theology, Biola University. Online: http://www.talbot.edu/ce20/educators/protestant/lois_lebar/.
Speer, Robert E. *The Finality of Jesus Christ*. New York: Revell, 1933.
Trumbull, H. Clay. *Teaching and Teachers, or, The Sunday-School Teacher's Teaching Work and the Other Work of the Sunday-School Teacher*. Philadelphia: J. D. Wattles, 1897.
Watts, Newman. *The Incomparable Book*. New York: American Tract Society, 1940.
Wittenberg, Rudolph M. *The Art of Group Discipline: A Mental Hygiene Approach to Leadership*. New York: Association Press, 1951.
———. *So You Want to Help People: A Mental Hygiene Primer for Group Leaders*. New York: Association Press, 1947.
Yates, Steve, and Larry Purcell. "Findley B. Edge" Christian Educators of the 20th Century. Talbot School of Theology, Biola University. Online: http://www.talbot.edu/ce20/educators/protestant/findley_edge/.

www.ingramcontent.com/pod-product-compliance
Lightning Source LLC
Chambersburg PA
CBHW070929160426
43193CB00011B/1631